# BAGHDAD MON AMOUR

Selected Writings of
SALAH AL HAMDANI

Translated from the French
by Sonia Alland

a Middlepoint Book
CURBSTONE PRESS

A Lannan Translation Selection
with Special Thanks to Patrick Lannan and
the Lannan Foundation Board of Directors


first English edition: 2008
copyright 2008 Salah Al Hamdani
translation copyright 2008 Sonia Alland

cover design: Susan Shapiro
cover artwork: painting by Ghassan

Connecticut Commission
on Culture & Tourism

This book was published with the support of
the Connecticut Commission on Culture and
Tourism, the Lannan Foundation, and
donations from many individuals. We are very
grateful for this support.

Library of Congress Cataloging-in-Publication Data

Hamdani, Salah, 1951-
  [Baghdad, mon amour. English]
  Baghdad, mon amour : selected writings of Salah Al Hamdani /
translated by Sonia Alland. — 1st ed.
    p. cm.
  ISBN 978-1-931896-44-3 (pbk. : alk. paper)
  I. Alland, Sonia. II. Title.

  PQ3979.2.H36B3413 2008
  892.7'8609—dc22

                                    2008008288

Middlepoint Books are edited for Curbstone Press by Sam Hamill


CURBSTONE PRESS   321 Jackson Street   Willimantic, CT 06226
        phone: 860-423-5110   e-mail: info@curbstone.org
                        www.curbstone.org

Translator's note:
I would like to thank Sam Hamill for his generous
contribution to the editing and composition of this volume.
I'm also most appreciative of Isabelle Lagny's fine
introduction and, lastly, want to thank my husband,
Alexander Alland, Jr., for his attentive and responsive
listening to the reading of the texts.

# Contents

# PREFACE

To read *The Crossing* and the poems of *Baghdad Mon Amour* in tandem is to be privy to the innermost thoughts of the poet, Salah Al Hamdani. In *The Crossing* Al Hamdani reveals the trials of growing up in Baghdad and the pain and confusion he finds in exile. He evokes the sights and sounds of the Baghdad he knew and that he may never see again. His sense of loss is poignant and ever present.

The trauma of exile, the memories and images it generates in *The Crossing,* then reappear in the poems of *Baghdad Mon Amour*. In the latter, however, the poet's inner world is imparted through the transformative language of poetry. And it is where Al Hamdani's expression of solidarity with the suffering of the oppressed is the most pervasive and intense.

In his exile, the poet adds other arrows to his quiver. He sings of love he has encountered: love that betrays, and love that heals. A father as well as a lover, he tenderly addresses his children. Indeed, he speaks to all of us, often with great wisdom. We also hear his cries of bitterness and, at times, sad resignation as he responds to violence and injustice. Yet, even in his moments of despair, we perceive a positive force that propels his writing and that, no doubt, has allowed him to survive under great hardship.

But after exile, can one return to one's homeland—and to one's family, in a sense, abandoned? In *The Return*, Salah Al Hamdani describes this experience, one of ludicrous complications and disturbing emotions. The *Poems of Baghdad* issue from this arduous, impassioned journey.

The literature of exile has found an exponent in Salah Al Hamdani in the compelling writing of *The Crossing* and *The Return* and in the evocative poetry of *Baghdad Mon Amour* and *Poems of Baghdad*. He is, above all, an engaged poet. In his work, he becomes a brother to those who rise up against oppression, employing the weapon of poetry to speak out against all assassins.

The last poem, *Farewell to Arms*, is a fit companion to the others and an altogether appropriate closure to these selected writings. It was written to honor a fellow militant, the American poet who founded Poets Against War before the U.S. invasion and occupation of Iraq began. Our writer reaches out to his comrade who, like him, confronts injustice through his writing. Just as Salah Al Hamdani is a brother of the oppressed so does he feel a kinship with another poet who shares his moral stand. There is no greater tribute he can pay to such a poet than to sing in his honor.

Sonia Alland

# INTRODUCTION

These are the poems and prose of Salah Al Hamdani, an Iraqi writer, a poet in exile. Written before and during the American invasion of 2003, they are a chant for the distressed people of Iraq, a hope for all people, civilians as well as soldiers affected by wars. After years of forced exile due to the bloody dictatorship of Saddam Hussein, this Iraqi poet condemned the Anglo-American intervention, a purveyor of innocent victims, which was being prepared. He analyzed the political situation from 2002, underlining the ambitions of the Americans. At the same time, in the media, he denounced the involvement of certain individuals in France with the dictatorial regime of Baghdad, but also spoke up against what he felt were the true reasons for the reservations expressed by the French government.

The 29th of March 2003, in Paris, during a nonviolent demonstration against the war, he and his companion were provoked by supporters of Saddam Hussein. The poet was then brutally assaulted by approximately twenty young Arabs from Iraq, Palestine, and North Africa, a group that had been moving among the demonstrators. He would not have come out of it alive without the help of other demonstrators who protected him as well as his friend. He, the defender of human rights, exiled in France since 1975, fell on a Paris sidewalk, under the blows of Saddam's supporters. Wounded, Salah Al Hamdani and his companion registered an official complaint against their assailants. A few days later, in Iraq, Saddam Hussein was in flight. The police and the Office of the Interior were no longer interested in the affair of the besieged poet, whose charges were classified without a follow-up. However, certain political parties on the left, as well as intellectuals, journalists, artists, and the Mayor of Paris, expressed their support for the writer. It was in this tormented context that the poems in the volume, *Baghdad Mon Amour*, were written. The newspaper *L'Humanité* published the title poem the very day the aggression occurred.

Salah Al Hamdani was born in Baghdad. The date of his birth, like those of numerous Iraqis, is uncertain. 1951 is noted on the State registers, instituted much later after the revolution of 1958. His grandparents were from the south of Iraq. His father emigrated to Baghdad to practice his profession as a gold and silversmith. A victim of unemployment, he became sick and died in the 1990's. Salah had no contact at all with his family during that period. Opposing Saddam Hussein and his regime in France, during the thirteen years that followed the invasion of Kuwait, he did not allow himself to call or write his family, fearing that doing so would prompt reprisals. His mother, illiterate but enterprising, was the determining element in the progress of the family. Salah, today a writer, the fourth of nine offspring, was, paradoxically, the only one not to have had the right to go to school. Was he already the refractory one he is today? The provocateur who can't keep silent before injustice? Thus he experienced a difficult childhood, which was that of most of the children born in the poor neighborhoods of Baghdad. To contribute ten centimes to the household each day, he worked from the age of seven at a hairdresser's. When he was eight, he was employed by a mattress maker, then by a car repairer. At about ten years of age, he apprenticed in an art foundry. He wore the *djellabah* and sandals, signs of his poverty, and began to frequent evening classes designed mainly for adults living marginal lives. Then he worked for a carpenter who built heavy doors that the young boy had to carry through Baghdad's streets to deliver. At around age fourteen, became a waiter in a café. The evening classes with their regular thrashings, at times by the teacher, at times by other students, were soon abandoned.

Intermittently, he worked as a water-carrier and street-seller of yogurt and candy. A mischievous and argumentative child, but never indifferent to another's suffering, he was soon resolving the conflicts in the streets that stirred up the bands of destitute children. A resourceful member of his family, he attracted little compassion from the others, but cultivated the love of his mother to whom he gave small gifts, in secret. The portrait that he draws of his father is that of a charming and humorous man, but who was also the cause of harsh disputes between them that were never resolved.

Without schooling and from a family of modest means, he had to choose an occupation. At seventeen, he joined the army. Thanks to his physical fitness and his moral stamina, he was chosen from among hundreds of recruits to be trained as a paratrooper. For four years, in Kirkuk in the north of Iraq, he was able, without being discovered, to liberate some Kurdish shepherds that the Iraqi army was persecuting and sequestering. Motivated, as always, by a deep sense of justice and fraternity, he rebelled against the arrogance and ideology of the Baath national party that dominated the army. Scandalized by the way the Baathists in the Iraqi army treated the Kurds, he joined a Marxist opposition group, rendered clandestine by the dictatorship already in place. While distributing tracts proposing a plot against the authorities, he was arrested and spent eight months incarcerated as a political prisoner. At that time, Ahmed Hassan Al Backer was President of Iraq and Saddam Hussein, a young assassin put in office by the CIA, was Vice-President.

The beginning of his detention was marked by long days of torture and a simulation of an execution. Nothing in his later writing refers to this trauma, as if the pain of the memory and his modesty over having shared it with so many other Iraqis who have remained anonymous prevented him from speaking about it. The traces remain on his body, however, and words spill out from time to time, in spite of themselves, destined for the ears of those dear to him.

After a hasty trial, the rest of his imprisonment constituted a second birth for him. He lived side by side with political prisoners of every stripe, all of whom opposed the

Baath party. They taught him how to think politically, how to play chess and, especially, how to read and write. A certain Yacoub, a comrade from the army who shared his cell and wrote poems, was his guide. With him, Al Hamdani discovered books and read the names and phrases of anonymous prisoners written on the walls. It was under these conditions that his first poem was born, which his friend promptly tore up saying: "You're crazy! You can't write things like that! Do you want to risk losing your head?" Salah came to understand the power of words as a result of this incident. He realized that writing was, after all, an honorable way of fighting.

Expelled from the army, he was finally freed from prison and found himself in Baghdad at loose ends. There was no work for this pariah marked for life by his army history. His family, constantly threatened by the Baathist police, asked him to keep at a distance. He settled in the Haider Khana neighborhood of old Baghdad, in a building filled with poor people and prostitutes. Of a bohemian nature, he wandered from one neighborhood to the other, from one café to the other, from alley to alley, looking for work, even if precarious. Often involved in fights with the militiamen of the Baath party who provoked him, he kept on the watch, ever ready to defend himself.

He discovered literature on the benches of the smoky cafés of Baghdad frequented by numerous poets and young Iraqi artists, who were readers of Rimbaud, Baudelaire, Al Marout, Al Sayab, Kafka, Plato, Marx, Sartre and, finally, Camus. He wrote poems during that period that he presented at competitions to official poets, who rejected them systematically. However, in his circle of friends and contacts, the young were particularly enthusiastic about his work. To get by, he began writing love letters for young people from comfortable families who were less inspired and less articulate than he. But that wasn't sufficient for living. The police harassed him constantly as did the fascist militia of

Saddam Hussein's Baathist party. When he escaped an actual attempt to assassinate him, his friends counseled him to flee to another country. But without money it was difficult for him to obtain a passport because of his personal history. He was finally able to leave Iraq with the help of some young people from the above-mentioned well-to-do families, as well as with the help of intellectuals and unknown poets who filled the cafés of Baghdad. Thus, one day, he left his family, his friends, and all his poems at the other end of the tracks and escaped.

Salah chose France because he was fascinated by the writer, Albert Camus, and his novel, *The Stranger*. Furnished with an official authorization to travel to Lebanon, he took the train, traveling clandestinely through Syria, then Turkey, and arrived in Paris in January 1975. Without knowing a single word of French, he wandered for two days with his bundle before finding his contact, a Tunisian of the political left.

As soon as he found his host, he was sequestered by him! Over three long days, he was subjected to a rigorous examination before being recognized as a friend and liberated by his Tunisian jailers. These same individuals helped him enter the University at Vincennes where he was allowed to register without a diploma in the theater department. Nevertheless, he looked for small jobs to support himself while he took evening theater classes at the University and, for several years, trained in the various aspects of that art form. In 1979 he was selected by the Argentine director Victor Garcia for the role of Enkidu in a production of *Gilgamesh* and was propelled onto a national stage, the Théâtre de Chaillot.

Other roles followed in the theater, the cinema, and on television. His political engagement in support of the Palestinian cause and of peace also found a place in his acting career with his participation in the European tour of a Palestinian troupe from Jerusalem. He took on the leading role of a play, alongside Christian, Jewish, and Muslim actors, retracing the history of the massacre of the inhabitants of a Palestinian village. Today, however, he denounces the kamikaze actions which have done great disservice to the people's cause and which, over a long period of time, received financial support from Saddam Hussein. His activism in favor of an Iraq free from dictatorship and the embargo, his vigorous support of Kurdish refugees from Iraq, as well as his involvement in labor union and other political activities in France, have occupied him more and more, necessitating a long pause, since the end of the 1980s, in his acting and directing career. He continues, however, to write poetry and short stories.

In the 1980s he was active as the representative of the League of Democratic Iraqi Artists, Writers, and Journalists in Exile in France. He was also cofounder, with other democratic exiled Iraqis, of the association, the Iraqi Forum.

While he desires a withdrawal, at some point, of the army occupying Iraq, he nevertheless vigorously denounces the terrorism being pursued by the Baathist party and the Islamists. He also insists on the responsibility of Europe in the present disaster because of its cooperation with the Saddam regime and its hypocritical and self-interested reserve in its nonengagement in the American intervention in Iraq. Ever faithful to his anti-imperialistic commitment regarding the American administration and his long-term support of the Palestinian people, he nevertheless denounces the present role of the parties on the left of Europe and elsewhere in the world in the rousing of an irrational anti-Americanism which will be of most benefit to the Iraqi and Syrian Baathists and, more generally, will help the Arab and Islamic nationalists, whether they be Palestinian or not, artisans of violence and regression.

As a poet, in 1979 he published at his own expense his first collection, *Gorges Bedouines* (*Bedouin Throats*) translated into French by the publisher Editions du Cherche

Midi. He was the cofounder of several socio-cultural associations and of two reviews of poetry: *Craies* (*Chalks*) 1980 and *Havres* (*Havens*) in 1982, as well as an edition of poetry, *l'Escalier Blanc* (*The White Stairway*). He is, at present, the author of more than twenty collections of poetry as well as of a book of short stories, *Le Cimetière des Oiseaux* (*The Cemetery of Birds*) published in French and in Arabic.

After meeting his present companion, love became a major theme in his poetry and French an experimental terrain for language, in poetry as in prose: *Ce qu'Il Reste de Lumière* (*What Remains of Light*), *Au Large de Douleur* (*Beyond Pain*). Existential conflicts expressed up to then in Arabic in a language of revolt that was ramified, agitated —*J'ai vu* (*I Have Seen*), *Au Dessus de la Table* (*Above the Table*), *Un Ciel* (*A Sky*), *L'Arrogance des Jours* (*The Arrogance of the Days*)—unfold now in French in a language more concise, in a more serene mood, still served by metaphor but resolutely turned towards the universal: *La Traversée* (*The Crossing*), *Baghdad Mon Amour, Poèmes de Baghdad*.

Isabelle Lagny (March 2006)
Translated by Sonia Alland

# BAGHDAD MON AMOUR

THE CROSSING

## So As Not to Forget

It was before the hail, before the seasons of war, well before
the age of man. My days of misery were not light-hearted,
but they were alive.

I first gave a sign of life at the foot of a bed surrounded
by jostling children. A bed anchored in a little room of a
house in the middle of a souk in Baghdad where several
families of modest means gathered together. This
neighborhood swarmed with lights, merchants, beggars, but
also with ruffians, spices and with those for whom love is a
business. With the arrival of Saddam and the assassination
of the dawn, my seasons have become orphans.

Madinat Al-Salam*, city of Iraq with a thousand and one
poets, from now on death will not find cemeteries vast
enough for your innocent ones.

*Madinat Al-Salam (city of peace), former name of Baghdad.*

## Alliance

Forgive me for having spent all this time in my room this year, in solitude, with this memory which, in spite of my relentlessness, hardly answers me anymore and hates me. I live with the expectation that one day it will predict my future. I haven't received any letters from my family in Iraq for a long time. My children don't speak my maternal language, and on the walls of my apartment there's no more space to hang their photos, along with those of the absent.

Today I was so overwhelmed by the realization that I started putting one postcard after the other on the mirror. So very many that there was no longer any space to see oneself in it.

Today is Friday and it's as if the telephone hasn't rung for several seasons. My heart is sealed with pain. I leave my chair and go out on the balcony to calm these palpitations, this anguish. Here, no port, no boats. No sail that moves off on a river.

I still have a full year before passing to the other embankment. I had better learn patience. My texts on exile, are they not audacious? I was so hoping that the coming days would permit me to cover the kilometers that remained before reaching the streams of my childhood.

I was saying to Alya in the car yesterday evening: what interests me are the events of life that acquire substance on paper when I write. I want to follow them calmly, without agitation. The style, the manner in which these things are said, are of little importance to me. Alya smiled, not saying a word, while I secretly dreamed of the southern wind of Mesopotamia blowing on my writing and carrying my breath away. I called for a soft and warm breeze to bring on the desert perfume.

For once I decided to walk with a light step. It was the hour of a joyfulness that little by little took on form in my head like a poem. Around me a host of happy days to be sketched out in the fog of winter.

January persisted with an icy frost, more penetrating than yesterday, and the echo of the days finished off the time of tears with a snarl.

In the past I accepted my exile far from Iraq very badly. Now, close to Alya, I like this waiting and this remoteness. I wanted to tame each stage of this solitude, in spite of the indifference of others and this stirring deep within me.

If ideas that create nourish the seed of their extinction, everything in this world runs the inevitable risk of disappearing. In other words, all will vanish inexorably in one last sigh.

To exist here still, with nothing from over there. To live here, while yet elsewhere, awkward perhaps, but it is living.

Suddenly, near the door that opens to the narrative, to men's cries, to the odor of childhood, a whiplash lacerates my throat. How can one emerge from within the book? I don't want to run away. Only retrace the days and remember with the soul of a child.

One never stops looking for oneself, risking, in the process, to lose oneself. Thus I never ceased fearing that my narrative would end up by burying me as if I were the last drowned person in history. Who knows what can happen during so many painful seasons of daily melancholy? I am the one who crosses a field under the evening rain and who remembers, over and beyond the grass, the echo of the dry seasons, the one who gazes at the clouds.

The Acknowledgeable and the Unacknowledgeable.

Last moments of winter. Final gasp of the day. Time carries away my world of yesterday. I feel my fifty years set down like bits of a broken mirror. I discover the muffled plodding between the acknowledgeable and the unacknowledgeable of those illusions woven around my life in a tight mesh. A half-century of torrents of regrets.

It is five-thirty this December morning. It seems to me I've been dozing during my entire exile and that I've just been awakened by the wailing of the Euphrates. Decidedly, the Euphrates' lamentation is too long to resemble the crackling of the frost or the moan of a lake in winter. It is thus that the cadavers accost the riverbanks thronged with my memories.

Nothing of note this morning. December's cold crushes, very simply, my day. My cry goes astray. I feel I'm growing older looking at the horizon, as nothing appears to want to divert my exile from its course. Happily there is this winter and this solitude in me.

With each new season, the fear invades me that I will never see my native country again with its clay houses and its shafts of palm trees. Inevitable tremblings of enigmatic days. Fear of finding nothing if I return there one day. Anguish of perhaps already having lost all. Those dear to me buried by Saddam, and the memory of my existence, evaporated.

It was the same when I parachuted from the airplane. I spun around and around and I thought my head was going to explode.

I hesitate to go far from my place. Perhaps it's because, instinctively, I recognize those who resemble me, those who forget the past is gone and the future is only an illusion.

Without question, I'll have to go out in spite of this black hole.

I came here to save my skin, so why not rewrite my history? But here's all of Baghdad being reborn in me and, with it, the malaise from a life that I left in tears.

Who am I? I'm a Baghdadian. A childhood in a poor neighborhood with streets too narrow, and nights littered with dreams. From very far, one senses dwellings closed in by silence. My childhood resembles an unending battle. From the age of seven, they sent me to work and, there, I wept away my youth. I'd go to sleep with fear, then the night would console me. Huddling near the rivers, the walls, and the fences of that pitiless life, I would revisit the suffocating dust of the workplaces and the brutality of adults.

I received so many blows!

In the heat of the Baghdad streets, I remember that odor of coagulated blood, those long treks in the dryness of the air. They made me do no matter what, as if they hated me. Then, trying to understand, I'd scrutinize the sky, the somber faces, and the bodies, with their dusty mouths, identical to mine.

Perhaps I didn't start truly reflecting on the meaning of my life until prison, when the voice of my tormentor resounded in concert, until dawn, with the torture of my body. It never occurred to me to call upon God's help since, in his name, one committed many atrocities. With my eyes riveted on graffiti narrating an imaginary life, I ended up clinging to the path of solitude. During those times they laughed at me. Worse still, I wasn't aware of the others' scorn.

At dawn, on the way to work, the sun glistened behind the brick houses jammed together on the horizon. Some workers would begin to assemble on the squares. Others would eat, sitting on whatever was handy. While their mouths chewed the dry bread, hard-boiled eggs, and onions squashed with blows of their fists, their eyes called upon me. The odor of tea mulled over embers and of the thick smoke rising from the flames of wooden cases and boxes invaded the nostrils of the sleeping city.

The end of each day resembled a nightmare. The arid heat provoked a fire on the asphalt streets. A child, I balanced a wardrobe door on my head in levitation over the city. Underneath, one was unaware of the exhaustion of my body bathed in sweat, my naked feet bound in the sandals of the poor. Years later, in July, my lungs still fill with the fumes from the tar. I could no longer breathe. I roamed the streets, waiting for the moment to die.

At home, late at night, the entire family would gather around a tray, faces somber but smiling, with an absent look. I would stare into my mother's eyes wanting to cry.

"This little one has got to go to school!" my mother would say.

"How are we going to manage if he stops working? Even the salary he brings home is not enough to pay for his needs, so what do you want him to do in that devil of a school?"

The next day would be like the others and, once again, I would leave alone at dawn...

Who will be my ally in this life? Father, why didn't you help me?

Evening classes were another nightmare. I left work around five-thirty p.m., taking the shortcut, in reverse, through the narrow streets. Incapable of being the little one that my mother had so desired, I wore a *djellabah* and sandals. I was like a man in the body of a child.

The years of my youth, more and more obscure, have become undecipherable. I grew up without an ally in the hostile milieu of adults. Survived, despite the distress, despite the blows received in the midst of wet tears.

To read and write with so little progress compared to other children of my age who went to schools for the rich every day. Sometimes, off by myself, I sneered at them. Actually, it had stopped being so bad. Later, I can't be sure any more.

The present was an abomination, it repulsed me. And yet I said very little about it. I didn't know what to think, what to say, and the future made me nauseous.

My time was punctuated with jumps and starts. As for me, I preferred to say nothing from the first jolts. Remain silent and look at the trucks passing by on their way to the frontiers. I never stopped listening, observing. But, at times, when the others teased me about my ignorance, I would lose my temper. Thus, back and forth, the streams of my life worked their devastation. I still hear them in me, like the rubbing together of bats' wings.

My life resembled a fall without reason. In that period, I saw myself forever engulfed in a world of fury with its dead, its cries, its dreams, and even its laughter. I didn't have a real job. I threw myself into any kind of work, not sure I'd be paid.

I subsisted. My days stretched out with no tomorrows, devoid of all passion. And yet, in resisting this world, I felt deep within me a throbbing for something else. Thus, I survived the disaster of my childhood.

In prison, after the army, the nights of study bore fruit: I learned to read and write Arabic perhaps better than the others. I tried to get ahead. With my questions, I always ended up finding my way, seizing the light. Digging further, without a plan and without a guide. My nights were enough for me.

Then one day, I sensed I was elsewhere, on ground that no one desired. Ground from nowhere, the size of my distress, of myself.

In that strange life, I felt the hideous pain of not being able to place things and beings at a distance. My despair, because of this incapacity, threw me defenseless onto men's paths; only my intuition would protect me later.

Today I'm truly thinking of changing course, swinging my ship about, going out to sea at the risk of mutilating my thoughts. Choose happiness instead of this jumble of a poor man's dreams. I want the resurrection of the body of my ideas, I want to escape my own handicap, lecture to myself, expose my indictment of dreaming and acquit myself. Is not happiness precious for a person saved from this long war against ignorance?

Whose Son?

"Goodbye," I say, handing him his suitcase.
"See you soon," he says, hugging me.

My friend Adil departed. I was at the entrance of the St. Lazare station. It was a January evening. I set out through Paris on foot. That evening I breathed in the rain, looking for traces of the past. The streetlights during those festive nights were of a vulgarity that tore at one's heart, but they served as guides to me. I had the foreboding of living a badly begun dream.

I remembered a foggy evening early in autumn when I was going to blend into the mystery of Paris. It was in 1980, before going to the Fontaine Theater where I was acting in a play by Copi. The neon lights splashed over the bars' facades. Posters of naked girls and prostitutes in flesh and blood punctuated the narrow path that led me to an entrance dazzling with light. Suddenly one of them called to me: "Want to go up, sweetie?" I played innocent, though, actually, her words excited me. She added, in response to my silence: "How about coming along with me, big guy?" That excited me even more.

The life of whores has always intrigued me. I see them as spontaneous, instinctive... Perhaps they remind me of my own wearisome life. Aren't we of the same kind? The only difference would reside in the fact that money doesn't motivate me. Indeed, like them, I've rarely been in love, and almost never happy... One must be ready to sacrifice in life, never say no...

The prostitute works without conviction but is always attentive to the other and gives of herself without stint... She gives of herself, then dies unknown. She is surely the incarnation of despair... the despair of the humble.

I was perhaps eleven years old when I met a true whore for the first time. She was my foreman's girlfriend. I was working in a carpentry shop in Baghdad where they made doors and wardrobes of hard wood. I have a vague memory of her. I've forgotten her name —and the name of my boss also.

The workshop was in Al-Rachid Street, in the tough neighborhood of Al-Midan. One morning, my boss asked me to take some money and clothes to his girlfriend who was at the city's central police station. He explained that I had to make believe I was her son so that I'd have access to her more easily.

Coming from the chief, an order was an order... In Baghdad one obtained what one wanted from hapless children. I fulfilled the mission with a certain skill and became for an entire afternoon a "son of a whore" altogether believable! My boss and my brothers in misfortune were astounded... Learning of what was to follow later in my life, one will no doubt consider this my first theatrical performance.

Later, I had to deliver some things to her at her residence. They gave me her address and I went.

As soon as she opened the door, she took me into her arms like a mother, then looked at me with a twinkle in her eye and latched onto my arm. Her radiant smile allowed me to hope and believe in anything and everything. There was so much tenderness in her eyes that, in spite of my age, I already imagined myself her lover! Then her look became enigmatic like the place she lived in.

Months later, I saw her by chance in Baghdad. It was four o'clock in the afternoon. I realized that she was waiting for customers with the other prostitutes. I was horribly sad. Up till then, I'd never realized what a prostitute was. I needed that spectacle to feel and understand that there was no amusement in it, nothing theatrical... That rendered me ambivalent towards her; I wanted to hurt her but I left. I'd suddenly grown up...

It rained so much during those long Baghdad nights... The ribbon of the Euphrates still carried the stigmata of the dawn's last tears... An infinity of tombs of my size. After all these years, after this flood, will the veil that hides the face of my days be raised? Will I finally understand?

At present, I'm alone on this sidewalk in the center of Paris. The city is a black hole. Exactly twenty-seven years ago— was it yesterday? —I came here, to this precise spot, in this station, the only survivor of an unperceived disaster. The many ideas I've gathered for so long are blooming.

Stand tall under the downpour of solitude, no matter what happens. The impression of coming out of a nightmare too big for me.

My instinct tells me to draw the curtain on what my life was like previously. What should I do with this fragmented past that, nevertheless, survives in me?

I'm heartsick when I awaken, sick of this life that I now judge tedious. This past that returns from the far distant steppes of my memory carries the bitter taste of absence and grips my soul. Yes, I hurt, and I'd like to cry out, but pirates have gagged me.

A child had laughed in a cemetery. It's Alya, my companion, who confided in me, with her discreet smiles and loving eyes, this January morning lost in fog. It was her little brother during their grandmother's funeral. Giggles overcame him when he saw a twisted old lady playing an organ in the middle of the tombs.

A child asks questions without listening to the answers. I sometimes wish for a world full of questions where I wouldn't give a damn about the answers.

The present has become cheerless and, in this fog, I celebrate an absurd event that makes me nauseous. It's often by taking shelter in a dream that I recapture a sense of tranquillity.

I have an incessant desire to change residence. I don't have enough money to move elsewhere. That's the exiled: he always wants to leave, change places without changing his skin. So, in order to flourish in his solitude, he marks his path with ideas on happiness.

I'm an individual without money who is trying to transform a miserable destiny into a joyous exploration. That can seem absurd. Perhaps that's why I feel lame.

When you left that morning, I thought I'd put a few things in my suitcase and return the key to my apartment to the project's office.

To renew oneself, it's often necessary to leave. For nowhere I say to myself. Never become attached to a place!

I've forgotten today how the idea of leaving Baghdad occurred to me and how I reserved a seat in a train for Istanbul, then for Paris. All those letters that have been sent to me for the past twenty-seven years and that I've hardly read are at present spread out on my bed with my solitude. The voices of their writers rise within me. All that ink, those words, which I inevitably never answered, reemerge out of a distant past. And if I returned to Baghdad now, my days and nights strewn on French earth, on the sidewalks, and in its stations? Only the risk of being killed by Saddam holds me back.

And over there, on the doorstep of my parents' house, a house I do not know, a sack full of these many years, this time of exile, and the face of an eighteen-year-old adolescent disfigured by wrinkles and gray hair. Confronting those who have disappeared, will I be absolved?

And if my return didn't surprise anyone, as if I were a child coming home after night school! How can I free myself from this diabolical anguish of being disappointed? What color will my smile take on?

Living with this anguish is baffling. Why would I go back, since deep within me I've never left Baghdad? At times one must simply no longer think about it.

## No One Knows Where the Day Goes

Once again, the night will provide no answers to my questions. Still perplexed about my behavior throughout the years, easy to influence and yet authentic, I feel imprisoned in an immense strangeness. I am banished. And if I were, definitively? I don't know what I want to be, but sometimes I think I've missed the train of existence from its departure, from my birth. What in the world can an exile's destiny resemble? My writings about an ill-formed life? After fifty years, I untie the packages of my childhood, I display my veins in an ordinary apartment, and I find nothing to say, nothing to write.

An edge of the silver moon vibrates to the rhythm of the clouds. I wonder if it will end up being stranded on my window, and I couldn't care less. This fragment of the moon doesn't know how to use her luster to draw a profit from the clouds and lets herself be carried away by the tempest of the stars. If I were a poet, I would compose a prayer whose verses would be destined for this sliver of moon. I would contemplate it like my mother when she was still a young woman lost within the destiny of my father's tribe.

I would have written fables about oppressed peoples as fashionable writers know how to do. I'd certainly have earned a good living. Everyone would have congratulated me. I would have returned every evening to my home, as proud as a rooster. I'd have been another "great" oriental writer with a red tie and a big car, admired by poor idiots.

January, of all the months, is the most favorable to storms, to afflictions and the wars of Bush, Sharon, and Saddam, those bastards, butchers of men.

After getting out of bed, leaving my room encumbered with pictures and books, I walk to where I'll meet a friend, a face.

Then, in this city, I finally give into the terrible punishment of solitude.

I, too, once had a country.

Since yesterday evening, I find I'm unable to look ahead. I have no desire either to get up, to talk, or to write... Some days I drown, I suffocate, mired in the past. Time marches on before me with its hazy sand dunes, with the feeling that these hours remind me of nothing more than my age. Behind the curtain, the hourglass has closed off time on the glass table.

In the past, voices clashed and overlapped the call to prayer. A street suddenly awakened by the arrival of the light at a gallop. Cries of street vendors, laughter of tellers of dreams and wheels that grind in this souk of Baghdad. It was as if the night's steed reared up suddenly before the rampart of the day.

After hanging up the phone that evening, I feared many things would have to be changed between us.

I saw myself like an ant going down the long hallway that separated me from the rain. What could it see of the sky and of the place where its path ended? I could describe what it saw. But could it do as much for me? What did it know about me?

The letter you gave me is on my glass table. I looked at the envelope the entire morning. I wasn't frightened of it. How can one fear the rain when one is already soaked to the skin?

What a *shitty mess!*—it's always those miserable words that come to my mind when I'm at a loss. It's of no matter to me this morning to feel the gentleness of the earth ravaged by the rain.

I think of my children, too far from me, of my people strangled by the embargo, the poisoned sword of Saddam over their heads. How can one feel joy when one is smitten by distress?

After several hours of silence, I decided to open your letter. I had to hold back a sob at that very moment. The word sorrow. You had written "Sorrow!" *Your* sorrow. And I and that ant, don't we have sorrow, we too, in this world of men?

I, who had sworn to avoid playing the role of the eternally unsatisfied lover, I now hoped for only one thing: that our bodies reunite as quickly as possible and that the tension between us be as fleeting as this morning shower. We'd then be able to laugh, the two of us, and our moments of sorrow would, in the end, fade away.

One night, in a train going to France, I was this guileless bedouin looking off in the distance at the lights of the big cities.

Already familiar with the difficulties of life, I lay in wait for the instant, within myself, favorable to the immensity of an interior frost.

I needed a misfortune that would give me the impression that I was accomplishing a heroic act, irreversible in the course of my destiny. The weight of the streets assaulted me. Hardly out of the station, I was thinking of my past and of the road I'd traveled.

Who could help me in this city? In the rain, the street stretched out before me with its pale and slippery sidewalks under a sky with no horizon. Farther away, I saw the Eiffel Tower rise up into the colorless dawn. The weakness of the daylight reflected the soul of its inhabitants. It was a little chilly, enough to prevent dreaming.

Drink your coffee with the break of day, poor devil. There's no hurry, you'll not be leaving all that soon. No, don't leave. Besides, no one will leave from here.

Drink your coffee, there's no hurry for a man who's living underground.

Those who are over there and who've never left, what have they become between the South and the North? In the beginning, there was only one condemned man who wanted to flee from death. Then others followed. And you, why did you leave?

Drink your coffee, as the day's beginning to single you out. Why did you leave while others resisted, and resist even more now, in spite of the immense silence of the days?
   The clamor of the dead no longer lets us sleep.

Drink your coffee. Don't go over there, stay in this country! Here, there's coffee and even something to eat if you want. There, one converses only with the dead.

Don't you know that here the memory of the innocent victim does not let go? It will never again leave you in peace. Imagine, then, in Iraq where the victims are counted in the thousands!

Drink your coffee. Outside it's gray, and they predict that our entire people wants to emigrate as the land no longer feeds them. Stay here, drink your coffee. Whether it's cold or hot outside, your coffee will calm your heart. In the past, before the advent of tyranny, before Saddam and his militia, before Saddam and his pirates, there was life.

Today, is it not a dead land?

Drink your coffee this cold morning. And think that perhaps one day you'll find yourself on an empty platform like old Sancho*, the Spaniard, his suitcase in hand and his soul trembling; you'll look at the train moving off, leaving you to face yourself, and sorrow will inevitably rise up in your heart. Yesterday when the peaceful Euphrates appeared unexpectedly in my room in the midst of palm trees, uncertainty invaded me. However, now that I'm at last facing this river, I experience the same sadness that flows like lava down to my knees.

*The maternal great-grandfather of my children. Of Catalán origin, he was a communist militant and a convinced antifascist, exiled in France during Franco's dictatorship. In 1974, after forty years of exile, he returned to Spain at the moment that I arrived from Iraq, as if to take his place. "Yayo," as he was called, died a few years later in the solitude of a true militant, abandoned by all, including his family.

# Praise

*For Baghdad, my mother*

Oh Baghdad! I wanted to come to your aid, garner your patience, save your house, gather in your tears, defy the horror, uproot your mourning and protect your laughter. But you see, I'm only good at raking up a child's dreams. Without ceasing, exile tracks my every step.

When will I be able to make freedom ripen for you?

At times I see you seated in the tomb, leaning against yourself. Alone, your mouth filled with dust, you are my other shore and I, your last echo. You are earth and heaven of my nostalgia. Alone facing your destiny, you scrape yourself against your own obscurity, for me, the moon's castaway.

And for those who have guided the ants to your body, am I no longer anything but the question mark behind your name?

In the past, Baghdad, I'd see you come and go in my room, I would revisit the destroyed houses, the disemboweled cars, the mutilated bodies, the broken faces. I passed over your warring flesh, then I missed you.

Your old age fades away like a look into the horizon. In this festive tyranny, you question the walls. Without news from me, you think of our past life, when you rocked me like a mother between sky and earth. How we used to laugh together then!

I'm standing at the window. The evening smells of the sea. I'm far from the path we took late into the imaginary. And yet, there's Iraq. A country without evening, without well-being, where there are no more lanes for lovers and where death stalks men, palms, rivers, and the moon.

So that Iraq may hear me, I have to unhook the words from my throat. When the Tigris and the Euphrates share my night, I'd like them to accept my nothingness, this minute reason for approaching them.

Before the Dawn

Still the little window, the glass table and the fragile silence pressed into the mirror. The day is sinking. The night will be cool, Baghdad is not far, and all is in readiness to trouble the memory of the bedouin in these unfamiliar cities.

I get rid of the room. My head swarms with people in mourning. What can I welcome to this place, apart from my things in disorder, my cumbersome body, and this almost obscene waiting? I don't want to unearth my words, my regret, this existence of a castaway, and nothing can divert me from the idea of going over there and squatting near those people ablaze in the morning light.

How to get out of this waiting when my mornings are like tombs, overturned by the tide of the executed who lament in my room?

My thought is a temple of desolation. How can I give name to the uprooting of the horizon, to desire and to melancholy? The light is so helpless in its understanding of my misfortune and yet so beautiful in its patience to break open this nothing.

I want to curl myself up with love, even in the midst of disorder, and write in the future tense to resist defeat.

The morning is dull, without taste, like deadened words in the eyes of an orphan.

Only suffering can unknot tomorrow's landscape. I'll have to skirt indifference, dispel weariness, readjust the target and draw the clouds over the earth desiccated by weapons. Walk barefoot on the coals of bewilderment.

Man of clay, condemned in the old days, one attaches poems vein by vein. One refines the writing. While I pass most of my time guarding the road of the palm tree, of the rain and of the bloody passage through Iraq, one tramples on the cry heard on the road taken by the castaways.

Since the funeral of Enkidu*, I had foreseen the defeat, but I'd never heard the song of the dawn. Then they put a price on my head before acquitting me.

This morning is like all the others. You've just left, without a train, without tracks, and without a destination. After an agitated night, walking down a path bordered with trees, I remain alone, riveted to my glass table, to my rhythm, to my history. I assemble the sentiments and retrace the distance covered. I blow into the coals of the storm asleep in the inkwell. I cling to the light, a gallop in the room. I finish off the unknown in a dream and let myself be gathered in by the void.

To be the guardian of this thread between the past and the present is exhausting. It's like drowning where one never loses breath definitively.

Rather than abandon one's body to others, it would be better to inhabit the silence, string one's bow, and not allow oneself to be fascinated by a sterile future.

The day is finally here, on its feet, ironic. Isn't it capable of thwarting boredom, men's afflictions? The seasons began some time ago and the harvests of the past are dreadfully ravaged.

Nothing remains but to play against oneself. The one who loses will be bound to the winter of others. He'll have flung himself, without a net and without a mask.

Love, struck down as well by nostalgia for over there, will be without a ship for this troublesome crossing. I'll join you splattered with mud, shivering, and consumed by solitude. And from the place of my imaginary death I'll speak to you like this: "…During a cold night, dew sprinkling the leaves of the trees, I see her dressed in white, led by four horses. Before the dawn, when, on the shore, one strikes the blows of my silent end, she will come. I'll bow down before her, sweet blossom of the chrysanthemum, I'll touch the palm of my hand, and, in turn, she'll caress the horseman dressed in transparency. I'll smile at her so that she'll understand my call and will warn my people..."*

It was a strong thread like love that fastened me to the country of death and to the days laid waste by barbarism.

Nothing has changed. Always the same window, the same glass table, the sluggish movements of satiated bodies, the rain denuded of sentiments. One must bleed one's thoughts, row without a shoreline, and always possess absence.

To dream in spite of this cold exile, to go out or to stay, but, all the while, dabbing our children's eyes with smiles.

Conqueror or conquered, one should provide for the future. One should persevere. Woe unto me if I must persevere with the howling of this dog in my head and the cold chant that rises from a distant childhood.

Oh my Iraq, streets of my youth, where are you?

Already noon. I am full of your sky, penetrated with despair of this life, my body, open, like a boat marooned on the sand. I measure the time that separates me from over there. Navigator, I count the islands in a book, the dead palms, and the seasons passed since we've been apart. The life of an exile contains many too many mornings of eternity for a winter hourglass.

In spite of this long labor, I wanted to harvest the instants, make a sheaf of the days, oil the rusty cities crowded with their inhabitants. Shake the old principles as one shakes an olive tree. Juggle with language. Strip naked our mornings,

*Extract from the poem: "Avant l'aurore (Before the Dawn)" taken from the collection "Gorges Bédouines," translated from the Arabic by Mohamed Aiouaz and Danielle Rolland, éd. Saint-Germain des Prés, Paris, 1979.

undress hope, reinvent our lost days. One must make of this life an art of loving.

Since bygone times, a child is born, an adult dies, a woman laughs, a mother cries, and thus, from a warm belly to a cold hole, all is inscribed for man. And here is the morning again, that eternal snare, when one wants only to be near one's love.

You, the woman with the antique face of the bedouin people. You, my palm tree, my minaret, my reed that dozes in the southern wind. You are the words of love and the secret prayer of the sacred cities prohibited to lovers. A man like me doesn't want a veiled language to express himself when the arms of twenty-nine countries plus those of Saddam have destroyed Mesopotamia, land of my birth.

Ever alone, I move forward. To conquer you, each day I'll trap my dreams, and I'll spread out, for yours, a fisherman's net. I departed a long time ago, leaving on a bench other writings, another sky, and all the words to describe a morning. On the doorstep of a house, I left a mother pursued by the derisive laughter of the days. I imagine myself the unique combatant assassinated in men's wars. Look at this hanging cord, these things scattered on the sidewalk and this body trampled by a curse. I'll not find my salvation if I don't succeed in purifying myself of this waiting.

When I returned home in a sweat, it was already late. The autumn had half frozen my years. My belongings were waiting for me, somber. How could I have lived so long with objects so foreign to me? When I turned on my computer and my green lamp, I finally recovered a paternal feeling towards them.

This time, instead of proceeding to my writing, I stood in front of the mirror. I took off my coat, then my shirt. Little by little, I found myself naked, except for this escaped prisoner's chain around my neck.

After the many years that I'd not looked at myself like this, was I still pleasing? My muscles were still firm, my vision had only weakened a bit, but time had labored my soul: the seasons had remodeled me. Hence, even my face had become strange to me.

I went to the keyboard. I'd not yet written anything when already the poem had taken form in my head. Wars, the dead, ruins and mutilations were waiting for me, as always.

My eyes fixed on the screen, I was aware of the position of each object in the room as well as the headlights of the cars moving outside the window. Intermittently I heard the harsh and vulgar voice of the woman living on the second floor that awakened my desire. And I hoped that Alya would return to me soon.

# Youth

Here's a poem from my younger years in Baghdad. I describe a boy, thin, slightly clothed, with torn sandals, and over him, an austere sky. This boy didn't associate with children of his own age.

The poem lying fallow, I settle down on a balcony overlooking the fish market, *Souk Hanoune*, a market teeming with customers, anonymous persons and pervaded by that foul odor which has made its reputation in central Baghdad. That year I'm in a sort of cavern. I listen only to my breathing and the burning of my thoughts. In this poem I put together huts made of palm branches planted in the red clay (a realistic image of the banks of Iraqi rivers at the time). On several occasions I speak of weakened men emerging from an imaginary camera. But the ink, my hands, and the poem don't succeed in seizing their image; it makes me weep. I project myself onto postcards from the war period, imprisoned in its absurdity.

In my neighborhood there is a tall stairway that the merchants' voices are unable to reach. I sit alone on the last step, penetrated by the emptiness, delving into my thoughts.

In Paris today, while my body rocks back and forth in the midst of lights and shadows, I cannot finish what I've started. I take notes in French without worrying about the pitfalls of the language. Could I be so sure of my style, so sure of my vision of things?

In Baghdad under a bridge, it was cooler. I stretched out on the red clay, my face spattered with flies and heat, and dozed. At times my adolescent's organ would harden and dig into the clay to chill my young man's soul far from others' eyes.

Today these memories haunt my body. My thoughts are no longer capable of keeping the secrets. My words are numbed by the assaults of winter.

How can I cry out my silence on the page?

Try to see a morning similar to mine
Solitude and a reluctant awakening

Try to have Iraq as one's country
And Saddam as a tyrant

Try to be surprised by a lonely cloud
And by a sky folded like a damp sheet on a balcony

Try to be the insurgent and the guilty one
Try to go back through the ephemeral days
Days that suffuse a morning
without leaving a trace

Try to be a factitious sword but one that cuts

Try to evade your memories
To disrobe your nights
To be the memory of the condemned one

Several weeks ago, I had a dream: I was leaving your place. The city was ominously empty. At certain moments of the past, it seemed to me that I could die like that. I'd die smiling, as if in a dream, my head slightly inclined towards the window, and I would groan, as if offering my body to death: death, which would not have come to take me had I not provoked it by offering myself.

When I saw you this afternoon, I said to myself that this idea of death doesn't fall in with the natural sense of things.

It doesn't represent my thinking accurately either. Couldn't it come up somewhere else but in a dream?

> My night is made of sand on a table of glass
> I have the odor of exile on me
> There is indeed my dwelling of clay
> Without garden, without forest or palm tree
> My sky is an inverted river
> And my words navigate
> Over a far-off country
> Where men look for the day's direction

Surrendering to panic, sometimes I call my morning a *shitty mess*. All my relations with time are summed up in cruel struggles, without executioners or victims.

Appalling. Yesterday, I went out in order to see more clearly in this night. To convince myself, I tried to battle with the invisible and prepared myself to be beaten. I remained watchful; in that way I would be ahead of the game...

I ran each night until I muzzled sentiments and pressed the clouds. That calmed my spirit. Then, on the way, the wound opened again and the pain returned... My life, agape, abandoned to waves, still and forever? And your own life, of what did it dream?

I would like to leave these places, to go off. I'm no longer able to maintain the stars' fire. How much longer must I trample my soul to erase the impasse from this crossing!

# BAGHDAD MON AMOUR

*Madinat Al-Salam*

Poems

I would like to express my deep gratitude to Isabelle Lagny for her part in giving form to this collection.

BAGHDAD MON AMOUR *is dedicated to those from here and from over there and to those who have departed...*

The Beginning of Words

I call to you in this white dawn bereft of snow. You who inhabit mornings like mine, who see skies like mine. For thirty years I've been trying to rejoin you with my exile.

My youth, my best years, I buried them near you. I counted them, I chewed and recounted them to forge memories.

My life in the past would have nothing of importance to relate. Before this plunge into your history, your civilization, my life in the Orient had no other form than the prison, than anguish and tears.

In 1975, my boat found a harbor in your city, on your streets. With your dogs, your poets, your writers, your artists, and yourself, my life took on the appearance of a dream. Then, how I dissipated my joy on the walls of Paris, on you, on your night and your mornings.

I wanted to lose nothing. To give without reserve, but waste nothing, to consume all, living for the moment. During my convalescence, after Baghdad, to accustom myself to the mother's absence, I wrote poems.

I followed the restless roads of all those years, a hail of cold crushed into bitter sobs. Those sobs from your stories then ran dry within me.

All the marble of the monuments, figurines, statuettes, effigies, Babylonian busts, my nights, my rivers, and my calls for sovereignty have been stolen from my body in the great souk of the Orient, by Napoleon-Saddam.

In my native country, one went to the mosque, one stood in formation before Allah, and one greeted the mother of the person one had executed with bare hands the day before. One nurtured lies, one kept Ramadan, the day, and one drank until drunk, the evening. The discussions of the sacred book were refined. The food was also. The dead and the victims were the color of the Orient sand.

There one was the unspeakable champion of the conjugation of the verb to kill: I kill, you kill, he (she) kills, we kill, you kill, they kill. One had invented the zero with the sole end of computing all the dead. We are champions in the way we choose between our cadavers and those of others.

I call to you from very far, from my cemetery and from those who died for nothing. I write to you from my fields of victims, from this bitter silence, from the cowardice of all the gods of man.

The hurt of living far from my own maddens me. Nothing of note menaces my night or troubles my malady in the deep obscurity except to pronounce the name of the steppes' light aloud:

Madinat al-Salam, Baghdad my love
I'm happy that Saddam, the butcher of your children, is dead.
Oh! Mother of misfortune, tell me what tormentor will come next...

In my room, the other evening, I smiled at an eagle come to keep me warm under his wings, spread out like a black cloud on a winter garden. My night is always the same— me, the silence, and this idea of possessing the day.

Baghdad, mon amour!

*Fever*

You know
last night
I gathered up all that was lingering in your memory
insomnia
the bit of bread
and the knife brimming over with sand

You know
the mildewed river
death fever
and your second silence
dawn woven with memories

You know
deep in that night
I gathered up everything
even your shadow
and the cadavers of my brothers.

## *Well-founded*

Though troubling
count among your exploits
the glory of not killing anyone.

## A Bit of Sky

It's a place
where scissor-cuts resemble saws
eyes don't fix on images of children
that fall into the waste basket
mine are in a heap where the leaves
the trees, the tears of stories
the skin of veins, drift into paper
into words of ink
trampled, to hurt
to make the clouds sob.

     And here we see my hand
     that flows into yours
caught
in the heart
to cherish the images
to become your tears
to reopen the box of bark
closed for the past twenty-eight years
to destroy the letters
to tear up the words
to create silence
to think about you
to penetrate your absence
desiring to please you
without uneasiness
just the dream of making you smile.

*Eleven—Arcueil*

The hearth of my soul
drowns in the obscurity of your choice.

Flame, howl your misfortune!

With the voice of the echo
the song of your frost is broken
without crying out
winter softens
your body in the hollow of the mirror
passage of my silhouette
your body misunderstood in memory
destined to voyage beyond the desert.

This wandering love
that winded your desire
leads to my shore, abrasive
and my exile emerges
in your distant gaze.

## Regret

These wild days that flower on the shores
of our mornings
I've picked them for you
day after day
and at present
all that remains are rifts
on the body of the evening
and a growing distress
thrust over the border.

The stories, resuscitated, arise from their sleep
set up a feast to futility.
Then
I hide my head behind the foolishness of conquerors
and I sing for blind walls
and for skies that are not mine.

You see
I don't possess the language
to  name the victims
simply
in my head
the tombs and the palms jostle each other.

Then
from my exile
I am alone each evening and fall sleep
with the dream of running tomorrow along the Euphrates.

## Ultimate

### I

To be for an instant a stone
without form or history
destined for an arrogant forehead

To have for a time fled from myself
to cross this dream-love
beyond all reason

For it's you who made me give way
you who were the nearest to my tree.

### II

At the bottom of this love for her
there is the uselessness of my hope.
And now today
she shapes her desires
she tramples the live coals of days
one gesture after the other.

If only you knew
how miserable we are!
Dust and water, our only fatherland.

### III

That night
Oh, the affliction my old solitude encountered!
Yet again
I had to pass with the scorching wind
on the wretched road of storms.

However
I saw myself knocked down like a wounded horse

and I knew, to live a little,
I had to bury that animal!


IV
Tell me, Liberty:
Who knows your unfathomable secrets?
For an eternity, martyrs have been questioning
and envying you
like those exiled behind the bars of their borders
who gaze
as they come and go
upon free men.

*To where you live*

We'll go only for an instant
to see the smile of my winter
and visit all that is yours!

Then...
chance follows its destiny
it settles in
and on your skin
irons out the consoled days.

Then your nights pile up
touching the cliffs of a dream.

What's important, isn't it that we love each other
a little, somewhere
like the solitude of dusk
sealed by a thousand eyes?

## Alike

If your heart has tired of telling the same thing
wait for me near the lilies of the valley
that house already occupied by someone else
enclosing our imaginary dwelling.

Yes
for years
I've consoled myself with a love
that's inescapable
and reflected on a war
I've not chosen.

## Sweat

Your love is happiness
I steal from the time of exile.
It blossoms on my years
like the laughter
of a barefooted forest
far from the fire...

## Revelation

Each time I think of Baghdad
I attempt to cry out
more loudly than my life.

Then return
the wintry days
and that palm dying in silence
on the margin of the page.

*Near you!*

I'm distraught that my eyes are closing, fearing that during
my sleep I'll awaken things that have been buried in me for
a long time: the assassination of the newspaper seller, the
photo of a young Kurd I had on me the evening I was taken
away, and the unbearable fear that God exists. My heart
shudders the moment my tormentor approaches my cell,
like thoughts of my mother that come to me with my last
breath. What have I lost with the disappearance of Garcia?[1]
And what did you say to me before our departure through
the mirror's frost? Tayeh, the dog, groans one last time and
awakens my childhood very late in the night.

1. *Victor Garcia, Argentinian director who died in 1982. The author
played the role of Enkidu under his direction in the* Epic of
Gilgamesh *at the National Theatre of Chaillot in 1979.*

*Flash*

Resting in a park
in the hollow of your hands
the day stretches out
like my desire
that you pin down
the horizon in your pocket.

## The Age of Reason

Double your day
divide your steps
be at the source of your inspiration.

Write with the language of your veins and your body.
Write for someone, for something, for nothing.

Write to go towards this nothing.
Temptation to redress one's emptiness, and the other's.

Write as if one were planting stones
in place of words.
May the words become palpable
like flesh
like two bodies under a sheet.

Be on the inside of things
never to the side
still less, looking on.

To be inside
is it not to be embodied in illusion
or in a reversal of oneself?

Be the target, not the one who shoots
be beyond yesterday, savoring the present
be life's equal
gnawing deep into the chest of time.

I saw a day that was cast
alone
on the roadway traveled by men.
That day led me closer to my desert over there.
Thus I divide the page

and accuse the horizon here of timidity
for bastards, they too have the right to a funeral.

I'm familiar with regret
I've known the executioner.
Today life is winded by absence.

Yes
one must dig roots for writing
displace the meaning
splatter it
thwart invisibility.

The dead fall far...over there...
beyond my table.

My dawn turned to face the other's break of day
that Palestinian child
frozen in the screen's morgue.

Should we not clear our planet
of those who assassinate
strike down beliefs
when it's a question of freedom?

Dictate light
vary the altitude, the sacred
walk and fall
but obstruct death
the world order, programming
nourish the man without purpose.

Die without a bullet, without a wound
convey that the hindrance is in one's self
and that heaviness plays no role.

Surprise the future, the immensity, the languages.

Pin words with your teeth
outside of the book
and conjugate conscience, knowledge.

If the pleasures of a tyrant exhaust you
don't give the echo a chance to modify your voice.
Never contemplate a tempest
that swallows up men.
Be in the tornado.

Despair always confronts the dispersed man.

A vagabond desert suddenly rises within me
an opaque nightfall
and yet my sole measure is love.

The future is a lie
when the victims no longer have enough blood
to staunch the flow of the assassins.

The cynicism of my time is skin-deep.

Forgetfulness, already...
rivals the age of reason.

Yes my love
morning discovers its light
like the dream its shadow
and because there's no more harmony without novelty
are you my ally at the overflowing of the dawn?

*Truth*

No one knows
the road that guides
memory
towards forgetfulness.

*Measure*

All of love could be held
in a streak of the horizon.

Reality is the mirror of things.

Death wins a little more territory each night
a surf giving birth to other sentiments.

This today is within your reach
and my memories
are plundered fields.

I also remember a country
a homeland behind barbed wire
and a valley like your body
when it falls asleep
and forgets what I've said.

## Contemplation

Emptiness
nothing but emptiness
when hand movements lie
and the body stretches
to face its story.

## Maneuver

You're not made of a tree
or a sudden shower
or frost.

Not born from night
from a stone
or from sand.

You were not born from me
giddiness
or from a slit in the sand.

Not born from a plover
or the trunk of a palm tree.

You were born from this echo from nowhere
from this immobile wind on the page
from this stray cloud above my head.

Epic from a foreign horizon
you were born from an hourglass
born from the color of rain.

Let the earth be unto the earth
all this is neither mine
nor yours
nor was it my ancestors'
or your fathers' fathers.

## Impatience

I've hastened
throughout the night.

The haggard light
and the day grow impatient
at the brink of my morning.

Ah! Baghdad
distance cools the air this winter
remember the words
composing your portrait.

In this voiceless exile
thick wall of waiting
there's a breach
the light passes
freed, perhaps, from its origin.

*Baghdad and You!*

If I were to meet Baghdad
at the corner of an alley
I would die from sorrow.

I've not forgotten
your hands
that are one with the piano
one with your look and the riverbank
and that cluster of distant villages.

## Baghdad Lapidated

### I

What palm tree will be reborn from scorched earth?
Baghdad, my writing's wound.

Ancient city
built on dust
remember:
we were born from your narrow streets
      when the star of the penniless
      was sung by the fishermen.
Betrayed city
unfasten our childhood from the terraces of *Al Rachid*[2]
and gather the guillotined palms
on the shores of your body.

### II

Violated city
you have nothing but the names of your martyrs on your walls
memory as revenge.

Orphaned city
I declare your injuries infinite
the cemeteries
from one hill to the other
make of you an open body
gaping
planted in uncertainty.

2. *Haroun Al-Rachid, first caliph of Baghdad who encouraged culture and the arts. His reign, in the history of the Arab world, is known as the "Golden Age".*

Oh Baghdad
cursed city
like you perhaps, I'll die among exiles
and I'll bind my tears to yours
and to those of your impotent gods.

*Testimony*

I've filled the days
with mouths sealed up

I've filled Baghdad
with roses and bread

And in the separation
where memories pass
I've not forgotten either the victims
or the chanting of the prairies.

## Warning

To take the inventory of the seasons
and imagine your morning,
Baghdad, I'd forewarned you
that to close one's eyelids
is to die
that to love
is to be alive
and that writing is an affliction.

Oh my tortured comrades
soon the good days will come back.

*Destributive*

Must I explain to you
what *Baghdad* means
and that reflection in your eyes...

Must I tell you
why one dies there
and this confounded bitterness
in my smile, at times

*Madinat Al-Salam*

I want you
perched in those wheat fields
to welcome in the evening

Wire stretched over the window of childhood
perfume of love crossing frontiers.

*Persistence*

## I

I'm ashamed
and on the road steeped in Baghdad's blood
my feet leave neither marks
nor shadows
nor light.

## II

In my room
the Euphrates is my flesh
and its laugh of long ago
a shore
buried in my hands.

## III

I live in France
far from the furious descent on Iraq
of birds of prey.
Oh my children
Baghdad is dying.

## IV

Who wants to join me
to wash death from our city
to reclaim its body
and its fleeing soul?

Oh my Iraq
memory dies in me
in bursts of light.

You are misery and yesterday's dream
you are the sudden grayness in my hair.

*For Fun*

The night is stranded on the roof
when the light wanders
in the nomads' desert.

Forgive me, my child,
if by mistake
I've hidden your moon
in my fist.

## At the Foot of a Fountain
*to my daughter Kermel*

What to write?

When age rusts words with a shower of looks
in the street
exile invades us.

What to write
handcuffed to emptiness?

What to invent
in the thickness of night?

What to say
when my absence has displaced language?

That solitude bursts in me
and that instant demolishes the dream.

Infinite
you and my image as a father

Beyond the frontiers of childhood
in your eyes
that do away with day, time, and exile
a silence unfolds
surrounding the dream of the fountain from long ago.

What remains of us?
A few silences.
Thus was I musing on the moment when
in agitation, you tried to win me over.

## Caster of Stones

By dint of hoping to see you again
I'm going to reconquer your dawn

I'm going to gather up the dates gorged with bullets
and my hands full
sacrifice myself to your light

The nights of exile
I'll throw a bridge of regrets over the river
and sow the enclosures.

## Happiness

When love
cannot make
the sign that consoles
why, at that moment,
does Baghdad appear?

## Tranquillity

There are thousands of days
over there
in my soul
where the tribes sleep

a desert is tranquil now.

*Tyrant*

Why, bastard, have you drawn your sword
over the dawn of the marshland men ?

Why have you destroyed
that morning perfume
and the laughter of the palms?

## Commitment

To the stranger
haunted unto death
by the scar of exile

To the mother without sleep
To the olive trees they assassinate in Palestine
To the captured palms from my Iraqi childhood

I say:

"We'll need a cord thicker and tighter
around the executioner's neck
to make him understand
the anguish of the victims."

## Idea

My life is submerged by cries of the tortured
The condemned overcome by solitude
leave at the foot of walls
their hair, their limbs, and their frozen screams

If I had to render my death lighter
far from you

I would make it compliant.

*Rule*

Cloud after cloud
the sun grows dim

War after war
man wears out

Leaf after leaf
the tree falls.

## Letter for the Absent One
### *For Isabelle, my Alya*

My beauty

Even if I've invented mornings
in rhythm with my dream for you
you illuminate lost landscapes
those immobile landscapes
that speak to us after the storm

Because one musn't imprison the sun
in a box
let us lay out the light on the wall
and continue to gaze at each other even from afar

You well know
daughter of the Aubrac
our love is a great field of rain
on arid soil
a great field of wind on the light of day

So I came to you
with all the men from the camps enclosed by barbed wire
that were unknown to you

From your look
I measured the future of my star

Beyond the living
I've loved you!

You're the humble river
where my past and its wounds find peace

I love you
like the shadow of a tree lost in a forest
like a winter
abandoned
to the great cold of memory.

*Wanting*

When
will I be free from tomorrows
free to live on the scale of the grand ending?

## The Heart's Load of Wisdom

### First step

When memories dissipate in the absurdity of distance and seasons from long ago have nothing more to say...don't panic, it's the heart that will take care of breathing into the soul the life of the most remote past.

### Second step

When one no longer finds love
in imagination,
one must let the heart
impose on the mind
its conduct.

*An Ethic*

Tolerance is the first condition of well-being
because it maintains the probability
that in the eyes of the other
there is a promise of fraternity.

## The Museum of Emptiness

When the days arrive
pain is vomited from the balcony.

Running is always difficult for the lame
and the deafening noises from the past
disperse Baghdad on imaginary dunes
laden with calamities
impatient to begin their feast of misfortune.

*Baghdad-on-the-Seine*
July 14th, 2001

You are dying like those unknown soldiers
under the horizon heavy with boredom
Baghdad
severed mirror
I'm alone in exile
the only one thinking of you

Baghdad
do not enclose the river
in your body
for I'll plunge into it
up to your soul

Baghdad
for the one who placed the kiss of death on your hills
and the one who wept over the abrasions of your heart
why this gray sky on your body
harvesting the silence
when I pronounce your name?

*Straight off*

If solitude resembles a lamp
If it doesn't light up your nights
you'll have to break it.

*Encounter*

The body of the moon
leaps at this hour
once again
over the tempest of past wars
and marks my regret to see your shawl
no longer hanging
over the years of exile

Your shawl, mother...
Mother...look at me!

*To an Almost Intimate Enemy*

Now that you know
this sad truth
that our weapons
are our martyrs...

When one morning you'll open your hollow memory
like the vulva of a woman without tenderness
one will signal somewhere the end of the camps for refugees
furious for having remained behind barbed wire.
From the slow-witted sleep of your spirit of that time
though surrounded by the tombs of martyrs
and cemeteries
a sigh will rise
and you'll at last understand what the poet was saying:
"One can uproot a man without slaying him"...

## Day Breaks Over Baghdad

Before the Euphrates there was a horizon
that guided the nomad
a tear over a dune
a shower on the cliffs
a hail of childhood
a light flooding the clay.

The Euphrates is my mother
and I acknowledge it
like one who moves quickly through his morning
to reach the sun's tattoo
on a palm tree
in an old courtyard.

*The Last Light*

This morning
the trees touch.
One must approach them as if on a pilgrimage.

One life joined to another
and overhead, a sky of smoke like a rope around one's throat.
Though our looks are proud
is not the story of our end narrated within us?

Before dawn, we'll leave in search of storks.
At the height of a man
we'll choose the best angle to see ourselves
but truth always arrives too late.
Thus we come and go again and again
on the road made of its corpse.

One of these mornings
we'll find the body of this life
naked
like a dry apple split in two
both halves lying
helpless.

Centuries later incapable of continuing
we'll sit down next to a lake
and share in its dying...

Our children grown
will climb the bridge of red clouds
to join convoys headed to a land of garbage.

Man
when you spread thought on clay
tying it to time
you write words of which ink is unaware.

Man
when your gaze upon the steppes
mocks peace dressed up with the body of words
you shackle meditation and the beauty of the past.

Man
when once again you pin your veins to this place
your mouth breathes life
within this destiny of marble.

Man
when you converse with history
so that its back is not turned
to the horseman with a luminous turban
you shelter the sigh of your village
fugitive moon
with the stone you throw at dawn
on the imaginary river.

You greet me like a rain shower?
Yes, my friend
I'm nothing but a cloud from the past wandering on the
sidewalk.

Man
when you resuscitate the memories of the peasant
who sang to your kind long ago
of the source of life
don't be an arrogant god.

Man
when you predict the end of the years of cement
how much longer must one wait?

And the cries of the children of Hiroshima,[3] of Halabja[4]
                            and of Jenin[5]
weigh today
like a flock fastened to our jaws...

We live at present by means of words
but tomorrow
what will we do with this century's enormous cadaver?

Man
when the distant years visit you
you train your shadow to withdraw
and when you imagine a childhood
which is not yours at all
you dry the other's tears in the day's dust.

3. *There were about 140,000 victims as a result of the atomic bomb the U.S. government dropped on this city on August 6, 1945.*

4. *Kurdish village bombarded with chemical arms on March 20, 1988, by order of Saddam Hussein. There were more than 5,000 victims.*

5. *Palestinian village that was the site of devastation and assassinations in 2002 by the Israeli occupation army (Tsahal) by order of the Prime Minister, Ariel Sharon.*

*Advice*

Look at the horizon
when you have important things to say

because it's beautiful!

*Before the End*
  *For Salah-Vincent, my son*

When I carry
the palm tree
to your desert
and to your feet
the foreign moon pool of rain
do not shed regrets on my tomb

Like the July wind
I'll lie down in the tall grass

Like the July wind of my childhood
I'll lament my absence at the foot of the steppes
and lie down like a mare that's been mounted

Then I'll say once again to the desert:
the cry that one perceives from a man
is always more beautiful than his silence.

## They Reinvent Death

This spring
between the emptiness of life and age
I move from place to place
upset by an overwhelming reality
and time steps over me.

Like an immigrant in haste
I straddle the years
my body resting in the corridor of the impossible return.

And if because of a fragile young sky
and the tragic posture of a fatherland in the throes of death
before one strikes again
history were to stop me?

*Mourning*

Which of us, oh Baghdad
knows the least of what the future holds
the Iraqi in great suffering before his executioner
or the Palestinian who lies under the tanks of pirates?

## Adorable Spring
*For Inès and Anissa, my daughters*

I hurry to plow time
to rummage in those ruins
that dust, the worst of aged shadows
to be found at the summit of an imaginary autumn
like this city lost in me.

My little ones
from my great height today
I see the evening a bit further than my age.
I've begun raining on your closed window
as before
and already the day of my birth is abraded
by the seasons of exile.

But as you know
you are my spring
so, for now, do not weep.

## Desolation

After all these years of searching for happiness
like a moth
you'll die in the light
after this hand you wanted to caress
shakes yours
and embraces you in condolence.

## Nightmare
*To my imaginary enemy*

In the beginning of November at midnight, I saw you put down a skeletal and faint moon at my door. Since then, you keep an eye on it through the keyhole as if you wanted something to happen. Me, I've watched it as one watches over a corpse. I've been on the lookout for you too, especially not wanting to miss your departure and fail to be the witness of the irreparable gesture of abandoning a poor moon in the middle of winter!

## *In Iraq*

When the walls tumble down
and their dust chokes the eyes
let the years from time past wake up at last!

The exiled will return in the midst of the storm
that makes all poems grow pale with desperation
and my unique desire
despite the assassination of the heart
will be that they keep their heads
on their shoulders.

## From Palestine to Baghdad

Steppe immense and harsh
where mirages gather
up to the distant caravan
where the wind's tears weary
but climb valiantly
to conquer my soul

lend your back to a fragment of the countryside
to display anguish
the sand reaching the dune and the dune
the horizon.

Stone hurled by a child of Palestine
I greet you
like a new moon over ancient Baghdad.

# Emergency

## The Origin of the Malaise

I breathe in the river and the corridor where I was lost
The hail on a paper sidewalk
The empty pool
and a sky over a vacant lot.

I breathe in the train abandoned in my room
The black bread, the egg,
The man from Malabar and the misery of my brother
The grass at dawn caressing the moon of childhood
And the litter of men in the country of solitude.

I breathe in ether in the city
A window inside the ear
The horses that pile up on the threshold of the morning
And the misty eyes of the mother.

I breathe in the winter in a hotel room
A field that buffets the horizon
Under the humid shirt of the night
And your dunes that ascend the length of your body.

I breathe in the malaise of your lips
In the web of love
Baghdad was like a toy
In the hand of an exiled boy
All night
At our door.

## Before Dying

*For Isabelle*
*Without her, life would not taste of the same serenity*
*And the horizon not be at hand.*

Early this morning I took off my memory
hung it on the door
and I knocked on the chest of time
like a peasant who digs a hole for the storm
like a mother wolf
penetrating in panic a forest in flames.

Soon
the chasm will stretch to the ocean
reaching the seasons of sorrow

Soon
the screaming face
and the language of flesh

Soon
in the eyes of the starving
desire will have a history
and hope will bathe their wounds

Soon
the laugh of the exile's mother will shatter the dawn of the
condemned one

Soon
we'll grind to powder the absence of days
the flight of truth
in the unbearable fall of men
    flood of calls
in a melting of blood

to tear away the decomposed destiny
and open the cemeteries to the unknown.

Soon my love
on the edge of a froth of writing
you'll plant my cry
on a tomb open to the sky,
on a life apprenticed to exile

In the thunderous sayings
of the one
in the fertility of ephemeral words from times past
of the other
in the burning hollow of ink
to live there
to die there.

November 27, 2002

*And Afterward?*

Under a taciturn sky
above herds wet from the storm
in a dawn, it also rusty
I skirt a destiny never looking for shelter from the wind
that wind that drives me to retrace
my ephemeral years.

And to say that upon awakening
there is a bouquet of dreams
for an encounter

and a season
that dresses your room in blue
driving dictators into the pit!

*The Habit of Exile*

From time to time
I contemplate the soul of children.
From their lofty height
Baghdad disrobes:
it has a memory, my memory
the palm trees impaled by wars
the bed where my father stretched out to die
the sky that opens onto the courtyard of the night school
and the moon in the sugar box.

Since then, the same morning perfumed with cardamom
wakes in my deserted field
the sad air tattooed on the walls of the city
and love stolen in the herds' dust.

You, Love, keeper of my sleep
like the habit of exile
I cherish you
So farewell mother,
over there
there's no longer a tomorrow.

*Words*

Who walks in me, worn out
when your wound allows no peace?

Baghdad
I'll divest you of your morgues
long in seizing
I'll divest you within the soul of things
from the depths of my childhood.

We have yet
side by side
to jump over
the delusions
of those doubles that gaze at us.

Will my memory still be unable
to decipher
the underside of things?

I want you
like a palm that every evening
turns giddy
curving its leaf-stalks.

We have yet
side by side
to jump over
the barbed wire of words.

For the murmuring of the dawn
where your rivers lie in wait for their prey
I was the stranger.

This shattered mirror
this fragile breath
this age
must contain our memories.

I like to think of you, Baghdad,
from without
from far away
from very far away
until intoxicated
seated by your side on the terrace of the Euphrates.

## A Preamble to Cowards

Before dying at the bottom of this page, it's most urgent
that I speak with you. Like the palms of Mesopotamia,
even more fragile than the inhabitants of the ancient Babel,
to die, I'd need only to incline my head towards the shores
of the Euphrates.

When the horizon of men catches fire

Do not fear losing your soul
In disrobing your memory
In denuding your heart
To dust
To reach cemeteries vanished in the tyrant's memory
Cherishing even the clay of men's earth.

Oh my children, at the edge of my words I sift the silence,
I catch myself dreaming of the fall of the most bloody evil
that my era has known.

Today I don't want to hide my words behind a life that
appears calm but thunders...

One must beware of words that accompany planes of war.
In the groans of a bleeding city's flesh, there is only
desolation.

This morning I want to renew my faith in man, the man
one has erased from collective memory, the one whose
thoughts will no longer spring forth. The man without
destiny, the one used like a dry olive branch to whip his
own kind and who thus contributes to the stream of blood
flowing from others.

The poet should not simply describe history to us, but
should witness what history has done to us, the men.

From what roots is made the assassin,
and me, my love, who am I?
How can one recapture the heavens lost in you?
I am also of that clay
clinging to the barrel of my body.

A light shower would have sufficed to be reborn from my
                                                  ashes.
Since your visit to the cemetery, my beloved,
I know that the wind, without warning, will steal the
                                          bouquet of lilies
that you placed on my tomb.

I come from Mesopotamia
from its gardens turned to dust
from its temples made tepid by time
where humans carry their cross!

What are they seeking throughout these stumbling days?
From season to season, here and now,
narrow openings, sacred books, sticks, shaved heads,
whips,
then generations that beg for upheaval.

You believe in all that's not seen,
I know, mother,
keep on weeping!

Late into the tireless night
when the sad day of the exile is soon to surface
never have I spread the seeds of the dead.

Already I hear the cries in the city
the inverted sky in the eyes of a lifeless child.

Hand to hand
one blow after another
I too scream
the fullness of my nerves
at the threshold of the page
bound to writing
my memories bow down before the eye's impasse
before languages
before the accent of your look
before this war of cowards
before the words of your body
until my existence is led astray
until my shadow is betrayed.

November 21, 2002

*Emergency*

To liberty I say:
we are behind the enclosure of time
behind the barbed wire of those barbarians.

To you, and to myself
for the war-conundrum
I'm going to tear the dead years apart
and cut the course in two so as not to escape.

To the companions of exile, become blind:
why scream into the valley of the victims' tombs?
I'll no longer tattoo bereavement on the bosom of history.
Only for their praise
and for those who'll die over there,
will I hew my words.

To you, and to myself
for the oppressed become grave-diggers of the innocent
with orphan stars
I've already decimated the limbs of children
on the road that devours the living.

Friends of derelicts
what's the meaning of an empty plate?
And on a table without tenderness:
a morning that never comes
a cloud on the roof
and a sun without men?

Friends, virile perhaps but far from those who are going
                                        to die
and whose grave and solitary trace my eyes follow
your festive mirage assassinates

for no one will exist in the cry of war
while you mirror yourself in our sobs
and stamp on our heart until daybreak.

Faint-hearted friends
after the ashes
I'll not dream again of the frozen river at the foot of the hill
I'll not pray again over my father's wound
nor on the shore of the streams from long ago
will I again drink the rain
that drowns the smile of the Euphrates.

January 1, 2003

## So Far From Your Sky of Metal
(Neither Bush nor Saddam)

All is ready
They prepare
faces grazed by a black wind
houses splattered with darkness
the souls of bastards as well.

All is ready
an immense metallic cloud
the assassins are on the banks of the Euphrates
the heavens have vanished.
Run, my little brother!

Yes my love,
you, like my other self
we, we know the generals,
their heads, their clothes,
their flags and their salaries
and their dedication
to cutting the throats of the innocent.

All is ready
even that moon reflected on my armoire
the broken mirror on the wall
my shadow in a heap on the page
my coat hung on the door
since the other war
and that dog limping on the pavement.

All is ready
people look at each other, cross paths
each faces his tomb, his truth, his virtue
for this war of cowards.

All is ready
To drag men to the slaughter
there's neither reed, nor God, nor palm tree, nor writing.
Where are the prophets, run, Mother!

There you are, my beloved,
we, we know the assassins
but the victims go nameless, always.

March 15, 2003

## Baghdad Mon Amour

Do not crucify yourself
not on the margin of a page
from a story that isn't yours,
nor in rhythm with the dead that enshroud your plagues
for nowhere will a cry comfort your pain.

Do not crucify yourself on the shores of the streams
that bleed your body
when the Euphrates suffers the secret of its soul
at the birth of a new defeat.
This I know,
not one wound is worth a war.

Do not crucify yourself at nightfall,
though you've not finished praying
over the bodies of the palms
for there are no honorable assassins.

Do not crucify yourself for the ash of calamities,
for the tombs of your Gods,
nor for the beliefs of a dying humanity.

Baghdad mon amour,
neither son, nor father, nor God,
nor prophet crowned by the church will save your soul,
nor that of Mecca,
nor the soul of those who refuse
to share the olive trees in Palestine.

Here is my notebook on the war
the years of exile
folded into a valise,
abandoned too long to the dreams of the condemned.

Here is my share of victims
my share of the moon,
my harvest of nothingness
my share of dust, of words and of cries.

Here is my misfortune
like a comma blocking the flow of ink.

Baghdad mon amour,
I crouched in the corner of the page
sheltered from arid days
far from torrents of blood
that carry off the name of the executed
and the silence of men.

Baghdad mon amour,
seated like a bedouin in a mirage
reclining on my shores, I cherished my own shroud.
Far from the cross, from the palm of Fatma
and from the star of David
far from their books, their wars
wandering in the sand of the dunes
from the steppe to the city
I drag my body from season to season
I haul you from the sofa to the mirror, from my room to the
                                                    street
between my writing and my solitude
sheltered from their cemeteries,
from their martyrs, from their morgues.

Baghdad mon amour,
do not tremble on the threshold of these fragmented days,
a civilization trained to kill
has violated your virginity.

Baghdad, city forever unsubdued by Saddam, your
                                            executioner
do not moan
at the simple revelation of this hegemony
those who agitate around your dying body,
those "liberators" are his accomplices.

Baghdad my wound,
my father labored and died without knowing joy
my mother lost her youth in the mirror
and the only witness to the first sorrow I wept on your breast
was the sigh of the sand,
and the starry sky and the eyes of God at the call to prayer.

Madinat al-Salam,
city of peace,
love in the soul of writing.

How I wish today
that man had never discovered fire
and I curse him for thus advancing
within his own turmoil.

This land that gave me birth is today put to death.
Oh, Mother! I want to rejoin your flesh
to listen to the pulsing of your soul
to quench my thirst on the whispering of your breath.

                              March 25, 2003

# All is Mine!

Will the day rise on a child's plaything?

In Commemoration of March 29, 2003[6]

> *For all the mothers of Iraqi exiles*
> *For the mothers of my children*
> *To my mother*
> *and also to Isabelle my beloved*

## (1)

*Against mourning!*

Over there they've muzzled mothers' throats,
Here, it is my beloved who's been beaten,
That body's timidity behind the valleys of the Aubrac
That glimmer of writing in the tree's shadow
That journal of sweat behind the frost
Lending savor to the field of stones!

6. *"An opponent of the Iraqi regime and his companion were shamefully put upon by a group of demonstrators carrying portraits of the dictator, Saddam Hussein, and the Iraqi flag. During the demonstration against the war Saturday afternoon in Paris, Saint-Germain Blvd., around 3 p.m., the Iraqi dramaturge and poet, Salah Al Hamdani, exiled in France, was responding to a team of television reporters. The writer was recognized by a group of demonstrators from the association, Iraqis in France. Young members of this association, more or less hooded by keffieh, in groups of twenty or thirty, have been involved in numerous incidents. Shakir Al-Saadi, president of the association, threw a first punch, followed by about fifteen other participants. Chased onto the sidewalk, the writer was twice overwhelmed by blows, one against twenty. 'It was a lynching,' he said, 'I did nothing more than speak in front of a camera. I can oppose Saddam Hussein and also denounce the war.' Firefighters came to his aid. Covered with swellings and bruises, both Salah Al Hamdani and his companion Isabelle Lagny lodged a complaint that evening against the president of the above-named association."* Liberation, Monday, March 31, 2003.

(2)

*The dogs of shame*

I name you daughter of the Aubrac.
Once again we were trapped
Among blows, claws, and cries...
Then on my tongue's bleeding road
Far from those passing by, I mended the sequel of my exile
Uneasy about the assassin sprung forth from my darkness.

There we were...
On the Paris pavement...trampled
Nearly lynched
Bitten by the dogs with the Iraqi flag
A flag drenched with the blood of Saddam's victims
Pummeled by the bullies of the Arab cause,
Those dogs of shame!

And there it is...
My reacquaintance with an old wound.

(3)

*A stolen instant*

In your bed in front of me the horizon is startled
On a window, this wall in my head
And the desert seems, with the infinite,
To unfurl within me.
The executioner is dead!

(4)

*The tireless path of the just*

Come, let us traverse the time left to us

Without a god who demands we make war

Without a sacred book that demands we cut throats

Still less for a fatherland
that doesn't nourish its children

Neither a tomb, nor a shroud, nor a trace
Nor a prayer for martyrs without a heart

Nothing for those Arabic-French dogs of Saddam in Paris
Neither hot coals for cold seasons
Nor light for assassins.


(5)

*The end of the road is in its beginning*

Come, let us warm men's winter
Carried off in a cart pulled by an old mule
toward another time
Let us contemplate the mule and the time going by
Dragging us from one border to another
From the bed to the window and from the window to the
cemetery.

## (6)

*Thirty years of exile to reflect upon the faces of the killers*

Frightened by the light of day
Saddam's dogs
Shield themselves under the mantle of shadow
Roam alone in the enclosure of days
Waste away with the hours
I know them...
I call them *assassins.*


## (7)

*A half-century and a few minutes*
*to understand men*

You, standing before the door of your past
You, the stranger in a photographic image
I don't want you to die on your knees
I am a celestial tortoise
My city is on my back
Come find refuge under my wings
Come, let us ride the dawn to find salvation.
Our executioner Saddam is dead!
You, the exile, I know you and I cherish you,
Oh my comrade.


## (8)

*One must not seek solitude when it's beautiful outside*

At the four doors of Baghdad
The men of red clay

Are like these days of Mesopotamia
That speak only of their suffering.
Me, I'm only one person,
And, in France, I want to speak of hope.

(9)

*My Iraq*

You are mine
Your mutilated inhabitants and your devastated land
The moon sheltered in the foliage of the palms
The fields and your metallic sky
And even that little upside-down minaret
Like a horse turned over on its back!

You are mine
The cemetery of the innocent
That tomb at the portal in the shade of the orange tree
That cadaver under the cart
And even the far-off star are witness to the smoke
Left by the passage of the airplane.

You are mine
From joy to pain
And from pain to the bleeding of your soul.

You are mine
The joy of a barefoot child who resembles me
runs now to catch the light
The enflamed portrait of the executioner on the pavement
Those sandals of misery by the thousands
Striking the mustache of the coward
And the sad gaze of the mother
finish off the night on the shore
where dawn moans.

(10)

*One must not listen to the angel*
*when there's such beauty in life*

All humanity is mine
Except the belief that doesn't want to cherish your distress,
Oh my Iraq
Except the writings of the heavens and their misfortunes
Except "Allah the great" of the starred flag
of the Iraq of Saddam and other assassins
And I, resisting this deluge of death
that swallows up my brothers,
Still.

April 19, 2003

# THE RETURN

*The Return is dedicated to those the assassins prevent me from seeing again. Those who saw me when I was born, hoping their children would see me pass away... My loved ones of the land between the two rivers who are still fighting with their tormentors!*

We'd just arrived in Damas. We left our suitcases at the hotel. First and foremost, the owner, the "Hadji," had to point out the shortest way to the "Sit Zeinab," the neighborhood where the Iraqis eat, do business, and get married in the traditional way. And because there one finds transportation services of all kinds. But before anything else, we had to go fishing for the freshest news about Iraq, for the reports the travelers brought back in their bags.

The taxi left the avenue, turning into a narrow street, and suddenly I had the impression I was once again in the Barbès neighborhood of Paris with its unbelievable assortment of people of all nationalities. Here, in addition, there were handcarts, and among the goods, presented any which way, were numerous souvenirs for the Muslim. The tomb of Al Saaïdi, known as "Sit Zeinab," is in fact one of the pilgrimage sites of the Shiite Muslim community. Street stalls, rather dirty, proposed *kebab* and *chawarma* that is eaten with the fingers. One drinks Iraqi tea— *tchauï*— and fermented milk— *elchininé* — while the voice of the muezzin mixes with those of the Koran readers, the street singers, and the lamentations of the Shiites. During the festival of *Achoura*, the Shiite Muslims strike their chests and backs with chains, paying homage to Hossein with their tears. My thoughts dry up in this racket. I'd really not missed it in these past decades. I'd quite simply forgotten it.

Ali, my traveling companion, insisted that we go to the office of a taxi company recommended to him. After some words back and forth, he ended by convincing me that it was the surest way of getting to Baghdad...

In this company's place of business, we fall upon a group of men poorly shaved, with mustaches. They appear bound together, some of them leaning against the wall, smoking. We greet them. They peer at us, searching for possible objects of value hidden in our clothes. They seem to take us for foreigners even though we're speaking Arabic with an Iraqi accent.

"Come in, please," says a young man installed behind a dirty, worn-out desk supported by crooked metal framework. He seems tired. We sit down opposite him. "Would you like some tea?" he asks.

"No, thank you," we answer, in one voice. However, a few minutes later, glasses of tea appear on the desk.

"Where do you want to go, I mean, where in Iraq?"

"To Baghdad," I say precipitately, before Ali can open his mouth.

"Only merchants have the right to cross the border at the moment," he says, studying our reaction.

Ali and I exchange questioning looks, then he adds: "One can also pass if the car is full of merchandise. The Americans are afraid of being killed, they're frightened of terrorists.

"What do we have to do with terrorists?" I ask.

Ali supports my point of view entirely, and adds, "We simply want to see our country again, the one we left years ago."

"Well then, you'll have to buy some merchandise. It's the only way to show that you're merchants. At present, there's no other way of getting into Iraq."

"But what kind of merchandise and in what quantity?" I say... "And if the Americans discover our subterfuge, what will happen to us?"

"We'll take care of that," he answers, sure of himself. "Don't worry!"

"So what should we do?" Ali asks him.

"You just have to pay me the price of the trip and of the merchandise."

He is silent for a bit, courteously inviting us to drink our tea, which, meanwhile, has changed color. Then he continues, "You pay in cash, please."

I understand that there's no other solution. My return to my country after thirty years of absence has an unexpected price. This idea of passing for merchants, camouflaging our identity and the true motive of our voyage is really absurd! Dark thoughts and doubts assail me. The fear of the unknown suddenly wells up in me. I'll perhaps die of a stray bullet *made in the USA*! After having escaped torturers like Saddam and his myrmidons, I'm to die today by the hand of the occupiers who have come, supposedly, to save my people from the dictatorship! I already have my head stuffed with troubling stories that people relate over and over again here. At times they tell you that the travelers are victims of racketeers on the road between Damas and Baghdad; other times one hears that the American occupier searches you before allowing you to enter your country and that, if he's in the mood, he may shoot you! The road to Baghdad is steeped in danger. One has to avoid being despoiled by thieves and assassinated by those who have lost their privileges, the orphans, the guerrillas of the fallen regime. After having fled from the occupier like rats, their method of defending the flag of the Arab nation and of Islam consists of attacking travelers! It was not enough to have pillaged the museums and the libraries, scattering the riches of Iraq as if one were shaking a sheet from the window of a top floor!

Before an onlooker like this one, who doesn't miss a crumb of our conversation, I have to feign reflection and conceal my uneasiness. With a display of body language and appropriate gestures while conversing on the side with Ali, I endeavor to present to our spectators an image of a decision taken in all seriousness, and declare finally that I'll pay. Immediately, we have to give the tired young man behind his wreck of a desk not only the sum of dollars indicated for the trip, but also what is supposed to pay for the merchandise, the nature and quantity of which I have as yet to be informed. We then agree that the departure for Baghdad will take place after midnight, more exactly at two o'clock in the morning. Finally we leave and rush into the heart of Damas on the lookout for shops and souks to buy presents destined for our families.

From that point on, each of us was preoccupied with resolving how to hide on his person, for the rest of the trip, the dollars he was carrying. We had to watch out for Iraqi racketeers, Arab Baathists who claim they're proving their patriotism by attacking unarmed travelers on the roads leading to Baghdad from Jordan and Syria.

I'd already spent hours perfecting a hiding place for my money in the double soles of my shoes. I'd glued the two parts with a German glue that would have discouraged any professional Saddamist thief, short of ripping apart the entire shoe to get it open. I hadn't revealed the hiding place to Ali, nor had I suggested that he hide his own money in his shoes. All his funds, he'd dissembled in the belt of his pants, but having forgotten to put some dollars aside for running expenses, he was forced to tell me and to ask me to advance him the part he'd need to pay for the rest of the trip.

Around two thirty in the morning, in the room of our modest hotel, the telephone rings. It's Hadji, the Syrian owner of the hotel: "The chauffeur who's going to drive you to Baghdad is here. He's waiting for you outside."

We throw on our clothes. Water splashed on our faces chases sleep away, then we go down with our suitcases to find the driver. He greets us, loudly imploring God's protection, hoping thereby to facilitate the crossing and assure us of a peaceful trip.

It was a full moon when the car took off toward the border. We were strangers to each other. It was Djallal, the driver, a somewhat obese Iraqi, who was to be our guide on our way to Iraq. He couldn't open his mouth without asking for God's help. Ali, an Iraqi and a Kurd, was living in France. We hadn't seen much of each other before the present. I therefore knew little about him except that he opposed my torturer, Saddam Hussein. It was through his older brother, a Muslim opponent of the fallen regime, that I'd made his acquaintance. He was also returning to our country but after only nine years of exile. It was actually the second time he was visiting his family in Baghdad. He'd confided in me that his first trip had gone badly. He'd been caught in a trap organized by his chauffeur, an accomplice of scoundrels. *"My second trip is more important than the first!"* he never ceased repeating. It was indeed a visit *that was going to change the course of his life*: he was returning to Baghdad for his marriage, and intended to take his wife back to France. To that end, he'd had to find witnesses, procure documents from the Consulate of France in Baghdad, and organize the preparation for the celebration, which would go on for days and nights.

Strangely enough, Ali did nothing but peacefully sleep in the back seat of our car in among packs of potato chips, and of his endless dreams.

A few hours before arriving at the border, I became hysterical with laughter at the sight of Ali curled up in that load of merchandise our driver had piled into the car. On the shelf in the back of the vehicle, Djallal had also stowed a large quantity of soda bottles held together with thick string, without forgetting to conclude his act with the inevitable, *"Inch Allah!"*

At the Syrian customs post, we spent several tiring hours, our passports in hand, held in groups in a series of rooms more disgusting to look at and to smell than a barn. Their dirty walls were adorned with portraits of "heroes of Syria," that is to say, of the tribal family, *Al Assad*. No one was to forget that he was in Syria, a Baathist state!

In the center of one room, secondhand furniture was enthroned. Seated at desks, the police did not speak, they yelled vulgarities. Not one document was allowed to pass without their feeling the warmth of baksheesh in dollars that, in plain view, they immediately slipped into their pockets. Normally, once one gives them the American bills, one receives in exchange the stamp of authorization to leave Syria.

After having passed the Syrian control post, we arrive finally at the place called *Abou Al Walid*, the entry port for Iraq on the road from Damas to Baghdad. We pass by lines of parked trailer-trucks stuffed with merchandise. They stretch out for several kilometers and thus appear to die on the outer edges of the road. The drivers stand on the asphalt, one after the other, in interminable waiting.

Weighed down by merchandise of every color, women and young people are there too. It seems as if all of man's sadness since the dawn of humanity is written on their faces.

"Where's Iraq? Where's the border?"

"Sometimes you have to wait two months before you have the right to enter Iraq," Djallal, the driver, answers.

Strange way of reassuring us! Perhaps it was his temperament. I don't react to his words. I desire only one thing: to find myself as quickly as possible in the heart of Baghdad despite the waiting and the danger.

Near the Iraqi control post, turning off the asphalt road, we come to an immense, unpaved open space. We park the car next to other vehicles assembled in this place, a spot teeming with people and dust.

"Give me your passports; I'll have them stamped," says Djallal.

His proposition makes me suspicious. How can I trust my passport to a person whom I've known for only a few hours? What would I do if my passport were lost? Though I'm also Iraqi, I have a French passport...

From my seat in the car, looking over at the control post, I perceive some Iraqi police, stiff as ramrods, encased within their silhouette. Youngsters or adults, they resemble each other so much that they must be from the same tribe. Their inexpressive faces evoke neither kindness nor intelligence. Perhaps they're bedouins, somewhat simple-minded, or Baathists, for they're growing mustaches to appear virile. They have the same faces as the demonstrators I saw gesticulate on Arabic and French television, screaming like servile imbeciles: "With our blood and soul, we sacrifice ourselves for you, Saddam!"

It's those people who will be inspecting my passport...Will they even understand the French? And if they discover I'm an opponent of their venerated Saddam, what will they do to me?

"We'll go to the control post together!" I say to Djallal. He makes no comment.

People of all ages wait, standing, the women in hooded cloaks, the *abayeh,* resembling a black cloud placed on the desert. The crowd jammed together in front of a barbed wire fence begins to call to the silent policemen who observe them from the other side.

I wasn't wrong. The police are armed with machine guns, revolvers and bludgeons. Most of them are bedouin kids about fifteen years old. They remind me strangely of the national guard, the Arab fascist militia of 1963 in Iraq. One of them starts to threaten the travelers with his revolver. It seems to me that after all these years nothing has changed!

"God be with you! I've been waiting three days for permission to enter Iraq," says a man who's carrying a little girl, frightened by the crowd, in his arms.

"You haven't a heart! How can you abandon us when you're Iraqis like us?" adds an old man.

"If you can't decide what to do, at least inform the Americans that we're here!" cries out another.

Suddenly the strident voice, rasping and violent, of a police officer covers those of the others: "I told you to move back, or I'll shoot! All you deserve is Saddam! You're nothing but dogs worthy of insults and the whip." His manner of speaking and his coldness frightened me. What is this language? How is he addressing people of our country that was, in former times, Mesopotamia? *May you be cursed, my torturer!*

The crowd, perturbed, disperses in bitterness, each individual wandering off with his worries. Djallal and I decide to return to the car where Ali continues sleeping as if nothing were happening. I then go off, leaving Djallal seated inside the car smoking a cigarette. He leans on the door left ajar because of the stifling heat. Without yet knowing precisely what I'm looking for, I start walking among people and parked cars. Perhaps I'll find a way of extracting myself from this place. What is the situation all these people are in? How do they spend the waiting hours and what are they thinking? Does even one of them have an inkling of a way out of this hornet's nest?

After only a few minutes, a man begins to scream. He's of medium height, rather puny-looking. He seems to have shot up from the dust. He says he's from Germany and, in his right hand, there's a video camera with which, while pivoting, he captures as much as he can. "I'm going to film you and send it to all the televisions in the world! To all of humanity, I'm going to be a witness of your suffering and denounce the inhuman attitude they have towards you. Look, I'm going to film the policeman who has a revolver in his hand!"

Indeed, a policeman is approaching the area of disturbance, pistol in hand, with the determination of someone who is going to administer the last bullet to the condemned who has just been shot by the firing squad. "You don't have the right to film here. You'd better stop that and shut up!" yells the policeman while advancing towards him.

"What right do you have to prevent me from filming?"

"Stop being an ass, or I'll break that camera over your head!" But the crowd begins to cry out: "No! Don't do it!" Someone speaks to the amateur cameraman: "God be with you! Why make problems for us? The policeman is telling you to stop filming, so stop! What's preventing you?"

A few minutes later, the conflict seems to have quieted down, the man has put away his camera. But the atmosphere remains tense. I have the feeling that, from one moment to the next, something grim could happen. I withdraw to walk among the trucks and passengers awaiting their departure. In this way, I manage to glean several stories from travelers who have witnessed events that would make one shudder. Thus, I learn that several days ago a woman gave birth at the border without any medical assistance and that a car, having forced a passage, exploded under rounds of machine gun fire...

Now I spot the German of Iraqi origin who's smoking. He's perched on a hill apart from the other travelers and the collection of cars. I approach him. "Hello," I say. "Their methods are bizarre, you saw how they treat the people."

"They're sons of bitches, cowards. They've never learned to address someone without threatening with a revolver."

"Did I understand that you come from Germany?"

"Yes, I'm originally from Iraq, but I have German nationality."

"What do you do in Germany?"

"I'm an industrial mechanic," he answers without hesitation. He's a unionist, that's certain. Here's an Iraqi worker who wants to provoke a rebellion! "Long live the unions, long live the Germany of the workers!" I say to myself.

"I saw everything that happened. What if we organize a demonstration protesting our treatment and succeed in making the American authorities come? What do you think of that?" While speaking to him, I stretch out my hand to shake his and introduce myself: "Salah, Iraqi exile of French nationality. I live in France and I'm a union member. If the Iraqi police have received the order not to allow us to pass, we should demand to see the Americans. They're the ones that decide, right? We have to conserve our energy. Let's not create conflicts with those sons of bitches, the Iraqi policemen. With their tribal mentality, they're nothing but crooks! How do you feel about it? I'm looking for people who think like me. Would you follow me, or not?"

He doesn't answer but looks at me warm-heartedly while descending quickly from the promontory.

I also turn away, to mix with the other travelers. I start once again to observe them and to think of a way of countering their fear. Suddenly my eye falls upon a little car. The bearded driver, with handsome features, is wearing the robes of Shiite dignitaries: a black turban and *djellabah* of the same color. He's playing with a rosary, black as well. I smile and think that to be Ali, the supreme Imam of the Shiites, all he needs is a sword!

I knock on the window. He lowers it amicably.

"*Salaam aleikum,* Master!" I say to him.

"Peace be with you. You are welcome. Do you want a little water?"

How could he guess that I was thirsty? Did he see it in my face?

"Master, why don't you come with me to encourage the people to demonstrate peacefully? We have the right to demand that we be permitted to return to our native land. Your presence is important to us in dealing with the Iraqi police. Today, you're an awe-inspiring symbol for the Americans. Your religious clothing provokes fear. They'll try to negotiate with you rather than insult you as they do with the others."

"I don't want to talk to the Americans. Let them do what they want!"

"Master, God keep you, it's not a question of conversing with the Americans but of finding a way to obtain a *laissez-passer* stamped on our passports."

He looks at me calmly, and with great interest, curious to understand the reasons for my proposal. "Where are you coming from?"

"From France, Master."

"Ah, from France! I have some good friends in that country!"

"They must know me as I've opposed the Iraqi dictatorship from there for years." I give him my visiting-card decorated with a dove, and joke, "Look, Master, it's the chicken of peace!" He shakes my hand, laughing, "Your idea of demonstrating is a good one, but how do we do it?"

"I don't ask you to do a thing. You don't have to talk, or raise your voice, either. With your prestige, all you have to do is precede us to that control post you see over there, next to the office. After that, I'll handle the authorities myself."

It appears that my idea has convinced the Master of the Shiites. Resolutely, he gets out of his car and locks the door. "I'll wait for you here until you give me a sign," he says, then he remains standing near his car, smoking a cigarette.

I head toward a crowd of men who are talking among themselves. I present my idea of a peaceful demonstration. But be careful! No one is to insult the police or throw stones like the Palestinians during their Intifada! Everyone is to assemble — only that — then let us, the Shiite Master and I, resolve the situation. I point out the dignitary, off in the distance, so that they can draw some courage from seeing him and explain to them that this person is waiting for nothing more than a sign from me to lead me to the control post. All we need to do then is to follow him. In this group, I immediately pick out a man who has the look of a fighter. While waiting to go into action, I encourage him to speak to other travelers to convince them to participate in this venture that poses no danger. I assume that the American in authority knows what a demonstration is. Perhaps he'll want to speak with us and will ask us who the spokesman of the group is. The Americans surely don't behave like the Iraqi police who only know how to threaten and shoot machine guns into the air. A police force that has no power of decision-making and that, moreover, isn't accustomed to demonstrations.

"Did you see how they insulted us? They treated us like cattle! We've got to have an American in charge come over here! I'm sure he's not far off. Perhaps over there in those tents behind the dunes..." I toss that off as if I'd prepared my union speech the night before. Only after an hour do we succeed in gathering enough men. But they're entangled in their *dejdaché* or in their pants. With their badly shaved faces and their protuberant stomachs, these people remind me of our demonstrators from the CGT in France. I signal to the Master who goes into action immediately. He comes over, taking a place near me, in the front row.

On the way to the command post, I discuss with him what I think would be the best approach: how we must express ourselves, the type of dialogue we'll have to conduct given what I know about the Americans.

At the word *American* he reacts vehemently, declaring with determination that he will be the one to speak. He, himself, will find the words that he considers appropriate. At that point we stop before a hedge of barbed wire facing the command post and the Iraqi police. A very nervous non-commissioned officer yells, "What do you want?" His vulgar tone makes me think once again that he's from Saddam's tribe.

"We want to meet the American in charge," the Master, very calmly and with assurance, answers him.

"We want to return to Iraq! We want to return to our country and see our families again!" the crowd exclaims.

The sand rises up at the slightest gust of wind. At the sound of the demands that begin to fuse in the burning atmosphere, police come out of a small house. They line up quickly, charge their rifles and aim at our chests.

I fear then that everyone will run away. Fortunately, it's not that way at all. Other groups of people, passive up to then, come to join us, and their demands flare up once again: "You're not ashamed to aim your rifle at your own countrymen?"

"Fire at us if you dare!"

"We shall die here!"

They are pressed so closely, one against the other, like matches in a box, that no one can predict what spark will set them on fire…

Finally, what I'd concocted ended up by happening: an officer advances towards us while returning his pistol to its holster and, in irritation, addresses the Master: "Master, what kind of demonstration is this? Do you mind telling me what's happening? What do you want?"

"My son, we only want a stamp that allows us to enter the country, nothing more. All of you should be a little more fearful of God's displeasure!"

"Master, we haven't the power to decide. We've been told to stay here and not to let anyone approach this entry. It's God's truth, we can't do a thing. How can you do this, you, who belong to the family of the last prophet? Go on, tell your companions to disperse before the American commanding officer comes and insults us all, you included!"

At that moment he signals to twenty or so Iraqi policemen who plant themselves behind him. Their bodies are stiff from the sun and ignorance and they literally swim in the American military uniforms that are too big for them. Those have surely not lost the habit of cutting off opponents' ears, tanning their skin, and burying them alive in pits, as under the reign of Saddam, their master.

"My son, you must understand that I won't budge from

here until the American in charge has come to see us. Didn't you tell me that he's the one who'll decide?"

"That's just the way you have to talk to him, Master!" I say, whispering into his ear while he proudly readjusts his cape and turban, the one just as black as the other.

"All right. That's enough. Now step back!" the Iraqi police officer says. And as we don't budge, he gives the order to the others to cross over the barbed wire and disperse us by force.

The scene seemed to have lasted hours. It was a ballet of human waves, rolling in and rolling out, melting into each other, growing calm and then, once more, tempestuous. I was in the middle of this moving mass with its sweat and its odor, and I contemplated the desolate horizon. *Is that really my homeland, that imbecile desert where men are thrown over the barbed wire of waiting and of barrenness?*

Finally what I was wishing for came about: a column of jeeps advanced, loaded with American soldiers. They placed themselves in a firing position. An imposing marine descended from one of the vehicles. His helmet appeared to be screwed onto his head and he was wearing dark glasses in a curved frame that covered his temples like a theatre mask. He was followed like a shadow by an Iraqi translator dressed in exactly the same manner, though he held his helmet in his hand, which exposed his shaved head, giving him a cruel air.

"What's going on?" screamed the translator in Arabic after having received instructions from his American superior. "Who's responsible for this ruckus? What do you want?"

"I'm responsible," I immediately answered, coming forward a few steps, as I feared this idiot would do something irreparable to the others. It would have made me regret my actions.

"And what do you want?"

My answer was for the group: "We want to return to Iraq,

to our country, and you're preventing us from doing it." I was addressing this Iraqi disguised as an American soldier with his banana glasses when a jeep approached me. Two Iraqis in civilian dress got out. One of them installed a television camera in front of me, while the other showered me with questions. "Where are you from?"

"From France."

"What do you have to say? Do you know that America is a democracy? You can say anything, don't be afraid, no one will hurt you. Feel free. We're going to televise your remarks, live, by satellite. Are you ready? We're filming!"

We were on the border of Iraq, however, not in America...The situation was becoming Kafka-esque. And I was in front of a camera, able to say everything, as in France on several occasions. But where does one begin?

I could have imagined anything except being filmed for television on the frontier of my homeland after thirty years of exile. Suddenly I felt consumed by solitude. I tested the stability of my legs to reassure myself that I wasn't made of sand, for I feared I would collapse on the instant and finish in the dust, as I was from that point on at a distance from the crowd, separated from the other travelers like a palm branch torn from its tree. How could that have happened? Why did I find myself far from the group of Iraqis massed behind the barbed wire who now were observing what was happening from afar? Would they be able to hear what I was saying? The Master looked at me with pride. I motioned to him with my hand in response. The Iraqi journalist continued questioning me: "Who are you, what are you doing here and what do you want?"

The imperious questions were shot out one after the other. They were disturbing, causing me to answer mechanically. "My name is Salah Al Hamdani. I'm a poet and have worked in the theatre. I've been in exile in France for thirty years... This is the first time I've returned to my homeland after this long separation... I don't understand why we're prevented from treading on our country's earth... We are being treated in an unacceptable manner... I've heard of painful things that happened here, a few days ago, to a pregnant woman. They say she gave birth at the frontier without even the most elementary care..."

Then I took a deep breath and swallowed hard before adding suddenly, "All of us here are Iraqis, not foreigners... Some of us have been waiting for several weeks... These methods used against the sons of Iraq are unacceptable. They're inhuman. We hope that those who are in authority will remedy the situation and change their attitude."

"Ah, you're an artist!...From your point of view, what is the solution?" the journalist asked me.

"The solution? Oh, yes, the solution... To tell the truth, these Iraqi police are just poor, ignorant men... Did you see how they're rigged out in military get-up that's too big?... Once more, it seems that they know neither how to read nor write but can only yell and insult the people... From my point of view, the solution is well beyond this frontier... The Americans should, as quickly as possible, hand over the power to the true representatives of the Iraqi people..."

"Do you have anything else to say?" the journalist started up again with annoyance.

"I want to go to Baghdad."

The journalist then asked the cameraman to pivot the camera and train it on those who had clustered together in the dust among the cars that were parked every which way.

I remained thus, standing like someone deaf, lost in a marriage celebration. I didn't know what to do. The entire crowd began to talk. There was a skirmish among the travelers and they started shouting at the police. Then other jeeps full of marines arrived, the soldiers concealed and ready for action.

The military translator with his black glasses in the form of a banana approached me: "Did I hear you say you wanted to go to Baghdad?" He spoke to me, then his eyes turned toward the others, and he added for my attention: "Is it true?"

"I've been waiting for this moment for thirty years, and I'm disheartened by it," I answered, nodding my head.

"*Yalà, rouh*: Go, then!"

I wondered if it was a joke, if he was making fun of me. I couldn't ascertain if he was serious as his eyes were masked by his strange glasses, dark like two deep pits. Two curtains of black glass, curved and glossy. My silhouette, in miniature, was reflected in them as if I were looking at myself through a telescope. This black crescent moon obstructing my questioner's face prevented me from seeing what he was looking at and guessing what he was thinking... This way of holding others in contempt, had he learned it from the Americans? How could he allow himself to say to me: "*Yalà, rouh,* well, go then?" What did he mean, *Go?* When we were hundreds of kilometers from Baghdad, without counting the years of suffering and separation that didn't have a price. Did he really think I could go to Baghdad on foot? He surprised and irritated me.

"Go where?"

"Didn't you say that you wanted to go to Baghdad?... So, *go!*... I'm telling you that you can go there!" And he showed the mirage far off behind the hamlets of clay houses, well beyond the villages and the solitary encampments.

"And my companions, all those people? I came from France with a friend. There's my driver, also, as well as all my things, and presents for the family."

"No, no, no, no, if you want to go to Baghdad, you go there alone. That way," he says, indicating, once again, the mirage.

"I can't do that all alone. There are others in this same situation."

He simply turned his head away, as if indifferent, and went a little further off to confer with his American allies.

He was then once more beset with questions by the crowd. This translator was strange. While he was circulating in the middle of the *dejdachés,* the *djellabahs* and the faces burned by the sun of Iraq, in spite of his Iraqi accent, he essentially contrasted with our compatriots by his large size, his American clothes and the whiteness of his face. He intrigued me beyond everything because of that and I didn't take my eyes off of him until his silhouette vanished into the crowd of Iraqis, and, with him, his glasses that reduced the human being to nothing.

When I finally left my place of observation to rejoin my traveling companions, there was a great scurrying about. People rushed to their cars. They were being allowed to set out again and pass over the border. They were heading in the direction of the mirage... I understood, at last, that the Americans had authorized certain people— women, children, the sick and those accompanying them— to continue their route. I said to myself: *It's better than nothing!*

Among those who had heard me speak, some thanked me. Others, on the contrary, regretted that I hadn't been of use to them: I should have explained their personal situation. Each one insisted on a special solution to his problem, but these same people, for the most part, had, precisely, done nothing. That's how it has been in Iraq for decades.

Nightfall arrived all at once and the cold took hold of us. I was then keenly aware of my fatigue and hunger. I'd eaten hardly anything the entire day. I hadn't washed or shaved. I hadn't drunk any coffee since I'd left Paris. I felt very alone. I thought of France, of my children and of Isabelle, my companion for life. I spoke to them from deep within me: *I didn't know, my beloved ones, what my destiny had planned for me on this frontier. Could Baghdad really exist in the distance, in that mirage towards which, without any chance of salvation, the soldier with the shaved head wanted to send me?*

I remembered shortly afterwards that Ali had bought three boxes of baklava in Syria. The cakes were meant for his mother and fiancée. In our car there were also about a hundred packages of potato chips and bottles of soda. I verified with a glance that they were still there. The packs of bottles were solidly stowed against the hatch in the back of the car. I said to Ali who had awakened in the meantime, "How would you like to give us one of your boxes of baklava? We're dying of hunger!"

"If Djallal can open the trunk, I'm not against it," he answered.

Before he finished speaking, Djallal had jumped out of the vehicle and was busy disengaging the bottles. A few minutes later, we threw ourselves onto a kilo and a half of Syrian baklava. Then we tore open packs of potato chips and drank bottles of soda, too many to count. I said to myself that it was surely the best way of having diarrhea at Iraq's border, in a place without toilets or a source of water.

Djallal, the driver, asked me, "Tell me, Salah, do you want us to take another road to cross the frontier? We just have to go back and take the route to Kameshli again. As for me, you know, I'm accustomed to driving long distances." He looked at us before continuing, "Don't worry, I won't go to sleep at the wheel. On the other hand, you have to realize that it will mean eighteen hours more of traveling, and you must add the price of gas."

"If need be, I can drive also, I have a license," I added.

Ali proposed his contribution as well. Then I said to them, "Let me think it over."

I left the car, leaving them in conversation. Outside, the cold whipped through me. My steps led me up to the barbed wire. On my way I discussed the possible reopening of the frontier with several travelers. Right next to the frontier post stood an armed policeman. I even went to question him about the Americans' intentions. He informed me that the frontier could be opened from one moment to the next without notice. "If you take what happened last night as an example, there were as many people as you see now. An American in charge came and gave us the order to allow everyone through, just like that! We don't know why they open and why they close. No one understands their logic. They couldn't care less about us. Whenever they decide, they only bellow, '*Go! Go! Rouh! Rouh!*'"

It was thus possible that they'd open the frontier in a little while, or in ten days, or perhaps never!

The policeman asked me, "Why didn't you take advantage of the chance to leave when you were allowed to do it just a while ago?"

I didn't bother answering him and drew away wishing him a good evening.

Returning to the car, I noticed a commotion that was unusual. I had the impression that everyone had decided to leave to try to cross the frontier at another spot. I heard talk of Kameshli where better treatment, it seemed, was reserved for travelers.

The Master was preparing to depart as well. He told me he was leaving this cursèd place. Before letting him go in search of a prayer rug from among the other travelers, we congratulated each other for what we'd done together for the others.

In the desert, when night falls, the dryness turns into a biting cold. Shivering, I got into the car where Ali and Djallal were continuing their discussion. "I think it's better to wait because the frontier could be opened at any moment," I said. "At daybreak, we'll probably head for Kameshli."

No one commented. Suddenly, Djallal sat up with a start and exclaimed, muffling his voice, "Traffickers!" He got out of the car and was lost in a crowd of men who were scrambling about in the obscurity. One heard voices that were almost inaudible:

"I'll take ten!"

"Give me fifteen."

"The same for me, please!"

"That's not enough, give me more because I've got a long trip ahead of me..."

A few minutes later, Djallal returned, "Do you have a few dollars?"

"What's that all about? Who are those men? Why do you need dollars?" I asked.

"They're trafficking gasoline," he said, looking annoyed.

"Where are they from?"

"They're relatives of the Iraqi or Syrian police, the young people from their tribes. They don't traffic only in gas but in all sorts of things..." Djallal's words were sufficient for us to understand that we were surrounded by those who sympathized with Saddam—racketeers and probably assassins.

I held out a few dollars for gas, but Ali and I thought it best not to leave the car.

At three o'clock in the morning the night was as dark as ink, blacker than tar. When Djallal returned to the car, we started talking about Iraq. Ali, though drowsy, was perhaps listening to us, still buried under the packages of potato chips.

At one moment or another we heard a discreet knock on the window and someone asked us, "Do you want to cross the border? I'll come by in a while for the answer. Fifty dollars cash if you want to get through with your car, understood? So prepare your dollars. I'll be back!"

Djallal remained silent at first, then said, "So Salah, what do you think? I don't have any money. I can't contribute. But if you decide to enter Iraq clandestinely, I'm not against it."

I looked over at Ali. "Well, Ali? What do you say?" Then,

without letting him answer, "Me, I'm for entering Iraq clandestinely. Tell me what you decide. Given the circumstances, each of us is responsible for himself. But I want you to know that if you're not willing to take the risk of getting in like that, I won't leave you here all alone."

"Fifty dollars for the car, it's not too expensive?" Ali said in astonishment.

Djallal said, "Of course not. There are three of us! If you count the price of gas for the distance and the eighteen hours of driving to reach the post at Kameshli, in my opinion, fifty dollars isn't much."

"Let's do it!" I say to Djallal, handing him the money... Still we must count only on ourselves, not get separated and follow the line of cars.

At that point Djallal started reciting a long prayer, exhorting the Lord of the universe to follow our path and to secure us against all dangers!

To ward off my fear, I pronounced, "Tomorrow, I'll eat our Baghelodhian bean dish in Baghdad! These idiots are too much!... So-called guardians! They're nothing but thieves!"


A little later, our car quietly started up. It was total darkness. We followed other cars maneuvering over mounds of sand. The cars glided one after the other, incessantly, and seemed to disappear into a well of black oil. Like blind people, we communicated in whispers and by touching each other. From time to time, we received instructions from individuals who were standing along the path. They spoke in low voices and gently hit the outside of the car. I had the impression we were surrounded by people who were observing us and guiding our movements while following the caravan formed by the vehicles. We couldn't see our car capering about but, surely, it would have been an astonishing spectacle. At times the moon allowed us a glimpse of the clouds of dust and the earth dislodged by the vehicle preceding us. Our car in the caravan dipped up and down over fallow land that was surrounded by the phantoms of clay hamlets, and those of the traffickers.

"Don't put on your lights!" we were instructed in an imperious tone of voice. "Don't open the doors, or the inside light will reveal where you are!"

We were also given orders not to bump the other cars, not to speak, and not to smoke. At certain moments, the car picked up speed. I was overjoyed. Finally, I said to myself, we're on a road! But in reality it only meant that we were on a slightly firmer and flatter portion of the way. At times the wheels skidded. We knew then that we were in a rut.

During this crossing, I had the feeling that I was wrapped in a shroud, placed in a coffin, and was being carried on the shoulders of a procession of phantoms constantly stumbling in the unstable earth and tripping against rocks in a field, freshly plowed.

The vehicles had already been advancing for some time in a long line of dots, two meters from each other, like the beads of a rosary. Everyone was frightened. Even the cars seemed to be. Suddenly the rosary broke and its grains scattered into the blackness. Where were we? In the steppes or in the middle of the desert? Once the line was split, the vehicles, as they went off in different directions, had surely gotten lost. Djallal the driver left the car to question the other lost travelers. But he forgot that, in getting out of the car, he would set off its inside light. That didn't fail to incur the anger of our entourage. His negligence risked provoking a catastrophe.

From within the darkness we could still see the small lights of the border post. What was startling to me was that, in spite of all the time that had elapsed, we were not yet far enough from danger. The frontier was there, so close, as if we'd never left! Then I remembered that in the dark, the distance of a light is difficult to judge. Soon a voice began to whisper in the blackness, finally reaching us: "I swear in the name of God all-powerful that if the Americans discover us they'll come in helicopters and massacre us!"

Another, in a low voice, agreed: "Of course, they'll take us for kamikaze terrorists who are trying to infiltrate!"

I heard these anguished voices that made my heart stop, and I immediately imagined running in every direction after having abandoned the car to seek protection in a hole, like a rabbit who jumps into a burrow to avoid the hunters' guns. But perhaps all that was only a strategy imagined by the traffickers to strip us of our clothes and goods and leave us here defenseless! Or even kill us! When the sun comes up, I'm sure the Americans will come upon us and we'll be captured. Then they'll give us the same treatment they give terrorists...

Other whispers came to our ears from all sides: "Should we go to the right?"

"No, no, no, to the left!"

"But why not continue straight ahead?"

I lowered my window to try to make out the contours of the phantoms who were moving excitedly all around us. Their heads were hidden by Palestinian *keffiehs*: *These are perhaps the same people who pushed me down and beat me in that Paris street last year when I demonstrated against Saddam and against the war!*

A voice interrupted my thoughts, asking all the travelers to get back in their cars and turn around. The right direction was, precisely, behind us. "How do we turn around in this darkness?" I asked Djallal. "Be careful of our backup lights, otherwise we'll bring on the American planes with their bombs!"

Just as we were experiencing the distress of being plunged into the unknown, muffled voices began to rise again in the obscurity: "Look at the light coming towards us! It's the leading car coming back. They haven't abandoned us, they haven't. Thank God! Thank God, we're saved!"

Indeed, an Iraqi police jeep approached us with three hooded men on board. One of them said, in a low voice, "Let's go, fall in behind us."

It's always the same thing with the border police charged with preventing undesirable traffic. It cheats the Americans today, as before, under the dictatorship, it did the Iraqi people. Lying, stealing, and trafficking are truly inscribed in their mentality.

As far as the Americans were concerned, the Iraqi police were supposed to be patrolling the length of the frontier to prevent the passage, during the night, of Arab terrorists. They certainly didn't suspect that the police, themselves, were responsible for illegal transactions and could indulge in lighting up the desert with their headlights in an extraordinary manner without worrying about the American presence.

The jeep rolled along slowly. We had only to follow it with our vehicles up to the main road, which indicated we were at the end of this troubled crossing.

That night, more than thirty cars loaded with merchandise and men passed under the noses of the American soldiers, crossing the obscurity of the Abou Al Walid desert without the least hindrance. Having at last reached the paved surface, they dispersed with tremendous speed, like water flung down nervously to the ground. Each car tried to pass the others, all of them loaded with travelers in search of their destiny. They spun off like marbles escaping from a bag torn clumsily by a child.

The first village we came to, driving down I know-not-what road, seemed abandoned. I was full of energy and completely awake in spite of the fatigue of the crossing. I had what force was needed to cling to life. Instinct was my guide in confronting danger. I discovered it later. And the sun, the lone star capable of preventing the darkness from remaining unpunished, had suddenly showered its heat upon us in celebration of the beginning of day.

Our car had not slowed down. On the contrary, it began to run furiously towards the horizon that daybreak was drawing above the road of deep black asphalt. It sped off and, like prohibited merchandise, piled up with our suitcases, our calamities, and our fears, we cut a rift through the desert.

My heart felt lighter and lighter: Baghdad was at the end of this straight line. I breathed in rhythm with the vibrations of the car. I gave shape to the horizon. My face was lost in the passage of the years and from my lips muffled groans escaped, inarticulate cries like those of a knight excluded from history. My head against the car window, I was overwhelmed by the feeling of being reborn. After an adventure where we had almost died, Ali, Djallal and I were safe and sound and I could almost see myself setting foot, at last, on my native earth. It had become a notebook that I used to leaf through to read the names of cities, rivers, childhood companions and that of my evening school. Then, after closing it, one ended up seeing the image of Baghdad on its cover.

I'd so tormented myself wondering if my mother would be waiting for me after the passing of the many seasons, and if I would read the dream on her face. How to be careful, also, of the clouds of *Fakhatis,* those migrating birds that would traverse my body at the moment I looked into her eyes?

It was still a long way to Baghdad. The husky voice, enough to make one cry, of a popular Iraqi singer rang out on the tape recorder, pouring out his nostalgia for the beloved he'd left so long ago.

I lowered the window, allowing my gaze to wander over the immensity of space, towards the unknown horizon that leaves its imprint deep in our eyes.

The infinite...

From time to time I heard the rustle of a handkerchief and the moans of Djallal. The singer's voice was breaking his heart. I didn't dare look at him so as not to disturb his solitude, his contemplation, his memories. Perhaps he was thinking of our frightful crossing, or he could, like me, be fearing the unknown... He lit up cigarettes and put them out, one after another. He could also be gripped by a sadness that left him unable to speak. He was muttering. With a mechanical gesture, he kept raising and lowering the window. He let his arm dangle outside to feel the force of the wind stretch it into a salute to the steppe with its scattered sheep and its herds of camels.

At the horizon, the sun erupted behind the dunes of rusty sand. A grand vision of a disk of red light slowly ascending. Coming from a mysterious place, it allowed itself to be drawn up toward an invisible chasm in the azure sky.

"Djallal, don't you see the magnificent spectacle? A fire that swirls in a vase and rises up into the void!"

We were speeding towards the light like a kite vanishing into the sky.

A little while later, while we were still rolling towards Baghdad, we began talking to each other, exalted by the events of our crossing. We readjusted our clothing. Hadn't we fought wild animals in an arena? We were no longer thinking about the dangers that, nevertheless, we should have apprehended in the bedouin villages scattered here and there along the road. We knew these villages were controlled by those fascist bastards that were entrenched among the innocent and disarmed inhabitants. The car started slowing down without any apparent reason. Djallal gently slid into a spot on the side of the road.

"Hey, Djallal, why have your stopped? I asked.

147

"Well, my friends, we are out of gas!"

We were dumbfounded. Without paying the slightest attention to our surprise, he got out to open the trunk. He took out a rubber hose about a meter long and an empty jerrycan. The hose was disgustingly dirty. The filth resembled a pile of insects stuck together. He went off a little way from us and stood in a place where he could be seen from afar. He then lit a cigarette, looking into nowhere. But no one passed along this road abandoned by everything, except the terrible rays of the sun.

"What are you waiting for, Djallal?" I said in a somewhat mocking tone, walking towards him in spite of a fear that made me look over my shoulder incessantly. "Do you think that people would be crazy enough to stop in this heat and give us gas? I'd like to see the person who'd take pity on us in this den of pirates and assassins!" My reproaches were born out of fear. "Why didn't you gauge the amount of gas that would be needed for the trip?"

Djallal kept smoking without a word, his eyes gazing into space.

"You were well aware of the distance to be covered, no?"

"Don't worry, the Iraqis stop to help those in need. I would do the same if I saw a car in trouble here." He smiled, drew on his cigarette and joked with me, "If we're attacked by Saddam's crew, it's bad luck for you. But if they're pirates, it's bad luck, especially for me!"

"You think that the Iraqis are still generous? You want me to believe that Saddam's politics and the endeavors of his henchmen haven't succeeded in stripping our compatriots of their humanity, of their inclination to sacrifice themselves for others?" I continued sarcastically, "In spite of thirty years of tyranny, in spite of wars... and in spite of the embargo?"

But he answered me with the soft and warm Iraqi accent that I knew so well: "Oh! Oh! What wars? The Iraqis' morale is still solid! The spirit of sacrifice and generosity is still supremely valued. Don't listen to all the slander that's meant to tarnish the honor of the Iraqi people."

I left him to watch over the emptiness with his jerrycan and his cigarette. Meanwhile I opened the Syrian newspaper I'd bought in the neighborhood of Sit Zeinab. Each page was full of articles on the Vietnamization of Iraq, on the Iraqi "resistance" by the people who it was said were, from north to south, in revolt against the American army.

War, destruction, and death had apparently invaded the Iraqi land. Its territory, since the American occupation, was nothing more than an immense cemetery. The same clichés were conveyed by the French journalists. Why all these lies?

I was overcome by sadness. Where are the American bombers? We were, nevertheless, in the center of the famous "Sunni Triangle" reputed to be resisting.[1]

Where were the resisters? Why weren't we seeing any of that? Though the Arab and international press speak of "Iraqi resistance," the ordinary people here consider these same resisters bands of thieves and assassins and, each morning, don't deprive themselves of cursing them out. A strange resistance that kills Iraqis before it gets to the occupier and works at destroying their resources rather than the American tanks. They're only the bandits of the former regime!

What was Djallal trying to say to me? Did he simply want to reassure me? Or did he really know more than I about the generosity of the Iraqis who had remained in the country? We, the exiled, we'd no doubt disappeared from the thoughts of those who had lived in Iraq over the volcano of the dictatorship.

At that instant, I noticed a car coming from the opposite direction that, indeed, stopped on the other side of the road.

---

1. *The conflict in Falluja started up again, however, a month later, in April 2004.*

Djallal ran across the road, quickly jumping over the security barrier in spite of his cumbersome body.

His youthful smile and his voice preceded him; he thanked the three individuals who had also gotten out of their vehicle quickly.

One of them opened their gas tank and Dajallal immediately thrust one end of the rubber hose he was carrying into it and put the other end in his mouth. He then began to breathe in as hard as he could, several times over, until he felt the warmth of the gas approaching his gums. At that moment, he seized his end of the hose and smoothly introduced it into the spout of the jerrycan that soon filled up. Everything happened before my eyes as if I were looking at a silent film.

A few seconds was all he needed to empty the contents of the jerrycan into our tank, then he got back into our car and started it up. He turned to me with a smile and said ironically, "They didn't request a *derem* for the gas! They said, 'It's our gift to you!' So Salah, what do you think about that? Did they stop in a dangerous spot to give us free gas, or didn't they?"

He became silent, lit a cigarette, then spoke to himself, full of pride, "That shit-head, Saddam! The Iraqi is still good and generous and he'll remain so in spite of history and our destiny! Hmph. Saddam influencing the Iraqis? That's idiotic! The Iraqi will remain what he is... Neither Saddam nor his henchmen will be able to change the Iraqi mentality and his legendary generosity."

Then his eyes burst with a smile and mine accompanied his with tears of joy, tears I'd tried to hide up till then by turning my eyes to the high palm trees that I perceived in the distance, trembling green clouds set delicately on a sailboat of sand pushed by destiny's hand like the drunken boat of Rimbaud. Then, without wings, the palms took flight over the mirage.

A little later, Djallal put the car radio on again and the melodramatic song of the Iraqi singer flowed over us once more. I was elsewhere, deep in my thoughts. My tears dried while the car carried us off on a road resembling a shimmering thread of gold.

Hours must have passed before the car finally left the highway.

"How about getting a bite to eat, my friends?" Djallal said. And accompanying his words with action, he parked the car in front of a building that seemed abandoned. It was an old gas station no longer in use, constructed of two sections, one in ruin and the other that was about to collapse. Over the entrance a sign announced *Restaurant of...* I no longer remember exactly, but it most likely had a relationship with the revolution or some battle led by our torturer. Close by, on the walls of a small store blackened by smoke that wanted to pass for a tea salon, we could read inscriptions traced in chalk and old motor oil indicating, I believe, *Café of Knowledge and Encounters.*

This place with its own life had surged up before us from the void in a desert metamorphosed by the highway with its mirages and its dust: a kind of restaurant about to collapse from one minute to the next, a coal-black café and three or four men with darkened faces. They raised their heads the moment we stepped into the dining room, their hands still plunged into the dish of *tachrib* full of rich, red tomato sauce.

"Come in! You're most welcome," said a man hidden by the door. From his massive stature and his enormous belly, I assumed he was the owner of the premises. The restaurant being almost empty, it was not difficult to find a table for three. I wondered where the clients for this place, to all appearances abandoned, could be coming from.

I ordered a dish of that famous *tachrib* that I hadn't eaten for thirty years. A soup plate arrived. In the center of a pile of pieces of dry bread soaked in tomato sauce was enthroned a large piece of mutton leg. This dish was eaten only with one's fingers and was normally served with lemon juice, onions, and vegetables steeped in vinegar. Before I was served, I asked the pot-bellied man where the toilet was. I envisioned washing my hands with great pleasure, as soap hadn't touched my skin since my departure from Syria. But when in front of the sink, I realized that the faucet was covered with a thick layer of filth and that the soap's form and color resembled a mildewed potato. Preferring to keep my own microbes, I was satisfied with rinsing my hands and face with water and drying them, prudently, on my T-shirt, then on my trousers. I had only to return to our table now. Facing me, I saw that the mirror was dirty also. It reflected a strange portrait that I discovered for the first time since I left. Was that really me? I couldn't go to see my mother looking like that! I had a gray, three-day-old beard and a blackened face. Had this trip cost me as much as thirty years of exile? I had the impression of having aged still more in three days.

I absolutely must shave and be the carrier of joy! What will my family say if they see me looking so abominable? "Djallal, do you know if there's a *hammam* on the road to Baghdad?

Djallal was wrestling with a bone in his dish of *tachrib*. He only laughed. "No, you don't need to get washed," he said, looking mischievously at Ali, who started to laugh with me while continuing to converse and eat.

A perfume of serenity must infuse my face, as if in preparation for the joy and the *youyous* of the first night of marriage. I wanted to be resplendent when I came to my beloved Baghdad once again, for I hoped she would be perfumed also, and adorned with the *kohl* of my thirty years of exile.

I didn't fear returning to Iraq even if, each day, I heard tragic news relayed by the French and Arabic media.

Today, those who wagered on the victory of Saddam's fascism have lost. He didn't render Jerusalem to the Arabs and the aircraft-carriers are still floating in the Gulf, while the Iraqi people remain alone to confront the occupier.

When one has no morals and no respect for life, one doesn't have a just cause to defend. I think that this principle should guide the victims even if it signifies nothing for their executioners.

*\*\*\**

My mouth full of that beautiful dust, I contemplate the landscape which, at one time, was simply an idea. The short-lived fruit of my imagination at present spreads out before me. It's a reality that, from now on, I can take hold of. It has nothing to do with my past dreams, nightmares sowed in the exile of my paralyzed mornings. Here on this generous earth, exile no longer has meaning and all eyes laugh and every heart beats for a new life. No more time for writing! No more right of asylum for solitude! Now, like the march of a people, men and things accompany me, like the moon and the night. Tomorrow, after so much dust, how will I be able to write to Isabelle of my love?

*\*\*\**

I walked for a long time from the street of Al Rachid to my childhood home that had become a carpenter's shop. In my neighborhood I noticed that neither the tyrant with his wars, nor the occupier, had planted a single nail. A terrible period in which the poor have only served as logs for the coals of war. Entire sections of the city with their men and their history forgotten by the movement of time.

Then suddenly someone cried out, "Come quickly, everyone, it's our Salah! He's back!"

Then a second person, tears in his eyes: "In the name of God! It's my childhood friend, I recognized his voice!...Salah! Why did you abandon us to this useless life? Do you remember that you were going to protect us?"

"Here's the neighborhood kid no one can forget!" cried still another.

My entire body began to tremble. Seeing them at loose ends, strolling down the street, I suddenly realized that the calamities that Iraq had undergone during all this time were of no concern to them.

The life of the poor is like a destructive war. It leads them, I said to myself, to their tomb, irremediably. It's true, the true war doesn't concern them. How should they deal, first of all, with their poverty? Whether it's the American occupation or the flight of the dictator and his miserable fedayeen who, nevertheless, have mistreated their wretched bodies, neither one nor the other troubles them. *Where is the star of my childhood? Is it really I who walk in the narrow streets of my neighborhood? Mother, if you only knew!*

During all those years of my life, I received no other visits than the sobs of the swamp birds, and only the wounds that guarded the threshold of our old house knocked on the door of my exile. The birds that perched long ago, exhausted, on the barriers of clay have also abandoned the terrace of the house where you would embrace us. How can I explain that today to my children in another country?

\*\*\*

On the sidewalk, a few steps from the house, as high as my chest, I raised the sail of my embarkation like a woman who lifts up her dress to cross a river. I folded my words, anchored their syllables to my lips. In the tumult of Baghdad, I coughed with all my strength and my throat submitted to the assaults of silence. I was a palm, asphyxiated by the smoke from explosions. It prayed for rain from a little cloud, a bundle full of dust in an airless sky.

*No, my torturer, I haven't finished asking questions. They'll never cease. Why would everyone already have plugged their ears when our existence is, in itself, no more than a big question?*

The palm trees have not grown old like me. They resume their voyage, in company with my sorrow, extending their branches now in greeting.

Though I don't walk on the water, I contemplate it, looking for a word on its banks. The Baghdad of former times, you, my delirious sailboat, my imaginary glory, let me cry out that the poem with which I attempt, in vain, to moor the Euphrates to the Tigris is pitiful. Despite the weariness of writing, despite the knife that is sharpened in the dark before slitting a throat, despite the insignificance of the Arab hymn and the echo of its explosion that enrages me, sad is the solitude of the man without a country!

*Don't seal the light of day under the eyelids of your dead. Think of the return of the rainbow that swirls about the tales for children to land on a prayer rug in a corner of our roof-terrace. Observe with a tender look and a child's joy the Aïd[7] and lost time. Don't neglect the mirror of our dreams; don't close the doors to dawn and don't lose our hearts among the pages of books. The absent one, the one who never ceased roaming in the melancholy of exile, will perhaps come back one day. Will he come back? He will.*

\*\*\*

Baghdad has fallen. The statues of the tyrant have been destroyed. And now what?

---

7. *An Islamic festival.*

***

I was observing my brother's eyes awash with the tears of the river, the reflection of the squat houses, and the shadow that floated above the great palms that issued from the epic of legends fixed in clay. Here he was, standing at my side, my older brother whom I hadn't seen for decades. He didn't have the black mustache that is the pride of certain men. They grow it to exhibit their virility, but render their face ugly. In spite of his age, his hair was not yet completely gray and his face expressed gentleness. That made me happy. His look was as nostalgic as the birds of the south. And now that my torturer was captured, I didn't want to disturb Jawad's serenity. He was following the flow of the Tigris, a river that seemed to be returning life to him. Then I very softly said to him, "Don't you think that America is occupying Iraq to prevent the Baath Party from being uprooted by the victims of the overthrown regime?"

And seeing that he was paying attention to me, I continued, "The Baathists should raise a statue to Bush in thanks!"

Before the fall of Baghdad, at the heart of the resistance of which so much has been said, along with the followers of Saddam, there were, indeed, some pockets of soldiers who sincerely wanted to defend the country. But they couldn't conceive of the macabre game played by those in command who, methodically, fled with Iraq's riches. The Baathists favorable to the regime thus abandoned the true resisters to the slaughterhouse of war.

My brother, silent, seemed interested, so I went on. "The Americans want to establish a base in Iraq to be able to strike the neighboring countries. Neither you nor I will be around when they depart. We'll have been dead for a long time!"

Jawad looked at me affectionately and started speaking. "What you say is perhaps true... but in Iraq, we don't think the way you exiles do. Most of us here want just one thing, to be able to eat and enjoy not having to put up with Saddam anymore. It's true that it's been decades since we've had any confidence in the political analysis made by Arabs or foreigners, any trust in the rulers of those other states that have abandoned us. But we especially detest those who assassinate in the name of God."

***

Today everything has become vague and mixed up. There's a feeling of loss, of being uprooted. At moments, despair takes hold of me and I have an unquenchable thirst to see my mother's face once more.

When I arrived in my old neighborhood, El Kefah Street, "the street of struggles", with my younger brother and my cousin, Bashir, the inhabitants surrounded us immediately. Everyone had memories, singling out the happy events of the past that were linked to these narrow alleys of our childhood. Strangely enough, I remembered neither the atmosphere of the neighborhood nor the look of its houses. What was most important to me was to recognize the faces of my old friends. I tried my best in the midst of sobs that broke my heart. There were also tears of joy and happy embraces. Then confused sentiments returned in Al Rachid Street where neither the statue of the poet, Al Rassafi, nor the café, *Oum Kalsoum*, that I frequented for years inspired hoped-for memories. The *Chanachil* architecture of my neighborhood houses and Abou Nawas Street were not familiar to me. It was then that on the slope of the Street of the Republic I noticed a little tree whose shadow fell on the threshold of a half-destroyed staircase. I recognized it immediately and I wept. It was my tree, now bare. It alone was capable of carrying me back to the days of my childhood, to my innocent moments of rest, long ago, in the shade of its foliage.

Don't our sentiments spring from our vision of the world and of being, from our struggles and our sacrifice for others? It's much more than an attachment to buildings and dust. This experience has reinforced my convictions as to the meaning of a fatherland and of sacrifice. What's the use of a fatherland if it doesn't nourish its people?

Around the word *fatherland* gravitate a quantity of slogans devoid of meaning. Not because they're obsolete or without emotion, but because they're not the result of thinking constructed, basically, on the needs of the Arab as an individual and his right to a decent life. They've been invented by tribal chiefs, ignorant and fanatical, who have proclaimed themselves chiefs by means of their cruelty. With the assistance of the West, they've installed themselves in power like thickheaded donkeys and govern the hearts of simple people. They never cease to retard progress and kick away the century of Enlightenment. Saddam and his Arabic nationalist party are an excellent example of this. They've dragged the inhabitants of Iraq to the slaughterhouse with all their might, have condemned their civilization to dullness and ruin. Then to crown their failure, they fled like thieves with their supporters, and all that was done in the name of the fatherland.

Iraq is surrounded by people and countries with rich land but where the present backward civilization lives by under-the-table dealings and lies. They're manipulated by patriotic slogans preaching Arab and Islamic extremism. And since the most remote times, this has not ceased to give birth to Arab tyrants.

In France, I'd never spoken of Iraq as a fatherland. It meant more to me to talk about the people who live in Iraq, about their beautiful traditions. About what they eat, how they pass the time, how they get together.

But two or three days after my return from Iraq, I felt torn apart and a terrible nostalgia overcame me. They were feelings that, before, I'd never felt imprinted on my heart, thoughts I'd never had.

In spite of the deep love I have for a woman of France and in spite of the presence of my children who fill my life with happiness, my existence here will, from now on, no longer be the same. At the same time, to live over there in Baghdad today will not bring me serenity either.

My distress can be measured by my attachment to the people from over there and to those from here, to my family in Iraq and to my family in France. I don't say *people* (meaning a nation) or *fatherland*. I want to call them *ordinary people,* or the *family.* Because the words *people* and *fatherland* burn like the names of gods. They don't have faces. On the other hand, *ordinary people* and the *family* take us back to their concrete existence, to life and death, to love and to human relations. That's why I was staunchly against the war, despite my profound desire to do away with the dictatorship.

Indeed, of what use is oil, sand, clay, water, the old Babylonian stones with which the Iraqis have ceaselessly built their houses, their museums, if it's to enclose themselves today with them behind barbed wire, in company with soldiers, and call that a *fatherland*? The Arab fatherlands of today, with their culture, their religion, aren't they actually concentration camps for their inhabitants?

*\*\*\**

When I decided to leave to visit my family, I ran up against the ambivalence of my feelings but also numerous difficulties. How could I, for example, put together the money necessary for the trip? I couldn't think of going to see

159

my family with empty hands. What could I offer them? What did they expect from me? Presents, money, medicine? After the dictatorship, the embargo, the wars, and thirty years of absence, I wondered what we might need at the moment of our reunion. Tears, perhaps? I had no idea. I was worried, anxious. I had become overly sensitive. A month before, I'd put the thirty years of waiting on a table and had turned them this way and that, examining them close-up for the first time.

For this trip, I'd decided to take a leave of thirty days from work. I wanted to do justice by those thirty years of exile. Thirty days without salary. Each year would be the equivalent of a day that I'd offer as a sacrifice to my mother. But, after that, where to begin? What was I to do? It seemed to me that the most difficult thing would be to explain my terrible absence, that quasi-disappearance from my family, and to have them accept it. My companion, Isabelle, was then the witness to my bitterness as an exile and to the existential anguish of my return. Just remembering that day hurts me.

Djallal the driver had taken us first to where Ali, my traveling companion, was to find his fiancée. "Their house is at the entrance to Baghdad. Yours is further, at the end of our road," Djallal said to me.

"For me, everything always happens *at the end of the road*," I remarked in a half-joking, half-anxious manner. And the car moved down gently from the bridge, plunging into the din of the city.

We unloaded Ali's baggage and greeted his family. We also wished him the best for the reunion party and his marriage.

Our car then turned around and reentered the interlacing streets loaded with vehicles devoid of license plates.

Baghdad resembled a cemetery of cars in the middle of which the donkey carts and Djallal's Jaguar struck the eye.

It was at that moment that my skin opened its pores like the windows of a chateau abandoned for many years, and there was a great current of air in my chest. At long last, I fixed my eyes on this city of which all that remained to me was the name. I felt assaulted by hallucinations and empty of emotions, sensing at the same time that my heart could at any moment escape from my chest.

All along this itinerary, I let myself be guided by the labyrinth of places and new streets. I looked at this city without features. In my head, however, were its ruins and the blood of its children.

"What is the exact address?" Djallal asked me. I articulated each syllable of the address for him as if it were another language. "I don't think we're far from your parents' house," he said matter-of-factly. He couldn't estimate the overwhelming effect of his words... "I don't think we're far from your parents' house..." With the weight of those words, of their sound, my soul caught on fire.

The tornado had dozed in me for thirty years. Like a bound and gagged hostage, I suddenly had difficulty breathing, my mouth half-open, waiting for the instant that one would undo me and allow me to dash away.

I'll be like the celestial bull, swallowing the dust of the houses, the streets, the palms, I'll throw off the weight of those years of exile and absence in the arms of my mother, a simple woman, with my tears.

The car left a wide avenue then turned into a street bordered by houses surrounded by gardens. It stopped, finally, in front of a metal gate. I got out and approached the enclosure wall. I looked over it for a moment and saw the front door of the house open. A large group came out and rushed to the gate. At that instant I didn't recognize anyone. I only became aware as, with tears streaming down my face, I was being embraced by everyone. Then my younger brother arrived and, sobbing, took me into his arms. I surrendered to his embrace in tears, as well.

Djallal didn't want to stay with us in spite of our inviting him to rest for a while. I embraced him warmly, as if I were saying goodbye to a brother whom, this time, I was leaving forever. Before his departure, I slipped a few dollars into the pocket of his jacket and left him the merchandise so he could sell it and get a little money from it. I also advised him, according to our custom, to take care of his health.

Once Djallal and his car had disappeared, the frontier and the crossing also vanished. I was then conducted into the house where, once again, I was enfolded with hugs and kisses. I was thus permitted to cross yet another threshold with tears, joy, and laughter.

This was, in fact, only my brother's house. Its interior was not terribly different from those of Iraqi families in exile, except that there were photographs of landscapes and suspension bridges as well as portraits of our Shiite spiritual leader, Ali Ben Abi Taleb, the son-in-law of Mohammed. That reminded me, suddenly, that I was born into a Shiite family. I had never been affected by the religion, and I'd altogether forgotten about it.

I couldn't swallow a single bite of the abundant offering of food set on the table.

I drank only a little tea and became acquainted with my brother's family. Among his five children there was a married daughter who was recovering from a recent miscarriage and who was pregnant again. My brother's wife and her family seemed like perfectly respectable people, though they were from Sadir City in Baghdad, a neighborhood with a bad reputation. It was this area that was called *the revolution.*

"I imagine you want to see our mother. She lives somewhere else, with the rest of the family. I'm sure you suspect she's waiting impatiently to see you again."

My brother finally spoke with her over the phone: "We're coming with Salah!... Yes, of course, he's here with us!... Yes, yes, safe and sound!"

When he hung up, he wiped away his tears. I didn't know why my big brother's tears intimidated me.

The older members of the family piled into a family car and the younger ones left on foot. I was behind the driver, squeezed between my brother, his wife, and their pregnant daughter. The driver, as far as I can remember, resembled a fish with a mustache, nicknamed Abou el Zoumer by the Iraqis. Next to him was a man with a child on his lap. During the trip, I looked at all of them out of the corner of my eye. They were overjoyed and, at the same time, in tears. Tears were also running from my own eyes, but I wasn't totally conscious of it. I suddenly began to imagine that we were all going to bury my father. Because of my exile, I hadn't been able to see him again before he died.

I couldn't understand where the strange sensation within me, the uneasiness and fear, was coming from. I was, at the same time, overwhelmed by emotion, and by emptiness. I also felt a shyness that wasn't customary with me. This shyness surprised me.

All of us understood each other, finally, with a single look. It's true, I said to myself, what do words mean when people haven't seen each other for thirty years? They appeared to be strangers to each other, and perhaps even to themselves, since the end of the dictatorship and the beginning of the occupation.

After a few minutes, the car stopped in a little street. "There's our mother's house," my big brother said into the air.

I said to myself, *"Salah, how can I hide now? Which way to turn? So there's where my mother and the rest of the family live. Will I recognize them? Will they recognize me? What do I say to my mother? Who can save me?"*

A god, a ghost, an angel, any being could have come to my aid at that moment!

It was the same feeling that had enveloped me before, when I entered my brother's house. However, this time I wanted to flee to shield myself from the eyes of those who were waiting for me. I was afraid of not being able to bear the intensity of the reunion with my mother. After all these years, what was she going to do?

I was scarcely out of the car when the door of the house opened and a cloud of black veils surged forth. People ran to meet me as if they were being chased by a fire that was burning them up.

How did they seize hold of me? If the energy of their frenzied kisses had been transformed into punches, I'd have lost my life. Their hands clung to every particle of my body. Words that I'd read in their recent letters about the absence of a loved one, about their sentiments of utmost love, were poured into my ears, onto my face and clothes, and submerged my being. I was weeping, unable to stop or pronounce a single word. I was encircled by women dressed in black, with hearts that were bursting. Yet where was my mother?

I was carried by the sound of sobbing, of *youyous* and of tears, as I made my way from the entrance into the living area of the house. It was then that I saw my mother. I simply went over to her and sat down near her. It was a few hours before I realized what was happening to me.

Everyone spoke, asked questions and wept, going back-and-forth incessantly, as was their way. As for me, as soon as I emerged from my absent state, lost in my memories of the thirty years of separation, I embraced my mother with great fervor. I started with her hands, then her cheeks and her eyes. Then, in tears, I threw myself into the arms of a brother or sister whom I kissed as ardently. Many hours passed in this manner.

Everyone was in tears. I was breathing heavily. I started trembling. Slowly I began to recognize the features of my brothers and sisters, of their children, as if I were awakening from a long sleep. Was I really sitting among them? Where had my thirty years of exile gone?

"You, my torturer, I curse you!" I thought suddenly.

"Do you want to eat or drink something?" My mother was addressing me as if I were a soldier returned from the battlefield. "My son, when you're tired, tell me. You'll sleep with me, won't you?

What did she mean? Was I to spend the entire night curled up next to her like a child?

I searched her face looking for an answer, but I came up against her glasses with large, thick lenses that deformed her eyes. My memory took me back to my adolescence. In the past, my mother overflowed with tenderness for me. "You're the one who will take care of me when I'm old," she used to say, in front of the others. Then, turning to them, she'd add, "I don't need you to take care of me as long as I have a son like Salah!"

When I was a child, what I earned from my daily work I would put into her hand at the end of each week. My audacious behavior made her laugh, and I would give her presents in secret. My mother was a beautiful woman. She was resourceful and lively and at that time did not need glasses. The shawl, that since I was born she never stopped wearing, covered her ears and all of her hair, allowing the emergence of a moon-like face surrounded by black cloth. A luminous face from the south of Iraq. Shy, she rarely raised her voice against anyone and in her simplicity was infinitely perceptive.

Living in Baghdad, in the capital, had not modified her attitude, that of a peasant. Her clothes were black for mourning, like those of all the mothers in the peasant families of my country. She was rather short and didn't look into the eyes of the person with whom she was speaking. She loved us all in silence and bore her pain in silence as well. She would weep, sad at heart, only in the middle of the night and, thus, allowed no one to penetrate the mysteries of her thinking.

I knew that she'd been waiting for me for years, that she would look for me, standing at the entrance to the street. They had told me.

I was at present sitting near her. I kissed her, while her eyes were lost in her own world, tears running now without respite down her cheeks wrinkled with age.

How could I sleep with my mother in her bed? A great embarrassment shook the years that have piled up as I've aged and provoked an explosion inside me.

What added to my worry about this strange proposition was that none of the others had reacted, had not been equally disturbed by the prospect. Was my mother suffering from a psychological disorder? Was she demented?

I kissed her again, my eyes wet with tears, but nevertheless I began to think of a way out while, at the same time, questioning my family about the past.

The light of daybreak was beginning to shine through the windows when my mother announced, "It's time to get a little sleep."

Everyone stood up and disappeared. I followed the shape of my aging mother enveloped in her clothes of mourning. That black color hadn't changed since my departure from Baghdad.

My mother entered her bedroom and I followed her, holding my breath, feeling faint.

"That's your bed," she said. Then, without further adieu, she slipped into hers.

My bed was small and plain and was opposite hers. At that moment I understood that my presence in the house wouldn't have satisfied her if she couldn't also hear my breathing in the night. She didn't allow me the leisure of warning her of my noisy snoring at night that disturbed the sleep of my love, Isabelle, and that of my children who were in France.

My mother had a unique way of sleeping. She rolled her body up in her black veil and buried herself in it.

For a few minutes, stupefied, I observed this immobile ball of black cloth on the bed. Everything I could see around me here seemed so simple: plastic flowers, a glass of water, a rosary, an old Koran, and a few boxes of medicine. Objects that revealed that the person who slept here was old. And that person was my mother.

From the time I arrived, everyone began going to bed late. Each evening they all yawned as they sat with me, fighting sleep so as not to leave me alone. We were going backwards in time. Our conversations, inevitably, turned to the past.

The days, the months, and the seasons merged to revive a memory and reveal a dream or buried suffering.

Even the saddest memories, because they were shared, became beautiful.

Each night, in her bedroom, I had a dream. It was always the same dream: the dead and buried from long ago would pay me a visit. They reproached me about my absence. My father, my grandfather, my uncle, as well as my grandmother and people whom I hadn't even known. Each time I woke up, I asked myself the same question: why hadn't these dead come to see me in France? I imagined the joy I'd have felt to welcome them, in the dream, into my room on the fifth floor of my building on the outskirts of the city. I'd have prepared tea for them, kept them in conversation until dawn instead of spending my time writing poems or solving problems for certain lazy Iraqi exiles.

But my phantoms were handicapped and a trip would have been risky for them because of the distance between Baghdad and Paris.

I think that even the most adventurous of them would have lost his way. What would he have done in France, not knowing how to speak the language or handle the money? And my address, how would he have found it?

I burst out laughing thinking about an Iraqi ghost lost in France without an address. But, still, in his forehead one could see the torturer's bullet.

I was becoming accustomed to relations with the living during the day and, at night, with the ghosts, until my mother proposed incongruously, "So, Salah, don't you want to visit your father's grave?"

"Of course I want to go, Mother. But don't you see the battle between Sadr and the Americans? That doesn't really encourage me to go to Najaf to visit my father's tomb or see the city! Sadr and his gang are over there! You can plainly see that they're using the sacred city as a shield. Isn't that exactly what our torturer did with the inhabitants of Iraq?"

"Yes, that's true, my son, that Sadr is shameless and has no fear of God. But you, you mustn't pay attention to that. Your father's waiting for your visit!"

"Mother, may God keep you well, but my father is dead. Where do you want him to go? Don't worry about the dead. They're not going to leave their graves. They have all the time in the world to wait!"

My mother did not comment. She nodded her head, her palms open, lifted upwards, to put herself in God's hands, and I saw anger in her wrinkled face. I had done nothing to deserve the hatred of her God. My presence, and its mystery, nourished a new day for my mother. My vision was too vast. I hadn't lost my time in exile treating the wound of my nostalgia. I wasn't satisfied with writing a journal dealing with my madness. On the contrary, with a pick in hand I'd rushed to be among the first to dig the tyrant's grave even deeper.

Accoutered in the mourning of mothers and widows, I'd licked my wound in secret like a cat to undo the ties that bound the wrists of my humanity… I knew that the admirers of the dictator would still be the first to profit, and the last to make a sacrifice.

***

This afternoon, my beloved, I send you my most humble, most tender words on human existence.

After such a long absence, I was frightened, so fearful, of that reunion with my loved ones.

The most terrible thing, after all, was the loss of the most simple bits of happiness right from the start of my exile.

Now it is three o'clock in the afternoon in Baghdad. There are still fissures among the clouds that allow the sun to spread its rays over the city. The streets are extraordinarily empty.

It seemed to me that the country had started to bark as guard dogs do from high on a hill near a sleeping village deep in the steppes. It was barking without respite as if to wake the inhabitants, and I said to myself that it was surely a sign announcing an extraordinary event. Then I changed into a solitary eye, leaving the world lagging behind me in the streets of Baghdad.

Why couldn't I sleep? Why did I awake in the middle of the night thinking of you, Saddam? Why does the Arab, my brother, always walk ahead, forgetful of everyone behind him?

One morning I was awakened by a noise. People were entering my mother's house. I heard scraps of their conversation in broken waves. They greeted each other out loud, whispering as soon as they pronounced my name. Then they started to sob. On the alert, I waited in my bed of insomnia for what was to come from their stifled words.

Some of them had been preparing dishes for me from the first crow of the rooster. I understood that they'd crossed the city in spite of the danger, carrying cumbersome pots on their heads. I sat up in my bed and, moved, looked up at the sky of Iraq through a window protected by bars. I got up, bewildered by the confusion of my emotions, with the pressing desire to write something about their generosity.

***

In the name of the same God, people can love, as well as fight each other. They can even exhibit the cadavers of their victims on their shoulders like blankets, in public, or in coffins that keep out the light and the cold dreams of Baghdad mornings. However, since I've arrived in this city, I've also seen the name of God in friendly places, in ruined houses that moan and that I'd abandoned in my youth.

***

From time to time, a guest of whom I had no memory would come to visit us. How many times did I wonder at the telling, then find myself in the events that were related in unbelievable stories from the past! Tales where comedy, arrogance, audacity and strangeness mixed together, resembling the narratives of those ancient books picked up at random to be read. Listening to these accounts, I was astonished at having known how to be of such help to those around me.

I found true serenity in Baghdad only in my old neighborhood. It was a muddy section, however, invaded by residue from the sewer, exactly as in the past when the level of dirty water, during flooding, rose to the neck of the bare-footed children. The mud flowing in a stream separated the rows of houses. Those that in other times perfumed the air with mint, watermelon, and cardamom had not moved. I remembered the pleasure of smelling the flat cakes of warm bread that my sister placed in the clay oven and that she took out, piled up, then separated and rearranged on large platters, leaving them where the small hands of those hanging about in the neighborhood could reach them.

***

In the morning, in spite of the brilliant sun, I had the feeling that my memory had just been abused. During the night, I roamed between the darkened passage of the hallway and the most remote room of the house while the light from the moon reflected dimly against the walls. In the sleeping house, at the sound of the wings of the garden crickets, I shivered like a sail tormented by a storm.

I couldn't discern the features of those who were pulling my body, like a fisherman's net, dragging it towards the haven of the Euphrates at the hour the river moans with its wounds between the threshold of the house and the palms bending over our hearts.

Baghdad, my gentle one, did you know how immense were my expectations of you? In my bags, I brought you cities covered with snow and made of paved streets trembling under the feet of demonstrators demanding your freedom.

I changed the years, the seasons, and the distances that kept me far from you into a great log that I began to consume, little by little, thirty years ago. Thus, by persisting, I am no longer, now, very far from your heart.

*** 

This house is not mine
This street, unfamiliar
But the nights are like those of long ago
And the sitting stars that guard the city
Wait in the emptiness
Like dogs without a master...

The door, ajar
My mother's silhouette
Despite her years
Bent over, at dawn,
At the hour of prayer
Lost among dishes
Cans of olives
Rationing tickets
Large sacks of chickpeas
Dust and war

As for me, the bird about to take flight
Nostalgia plucks at my soul
Like the victim of the torturer

Like the panther
I hold my flesh between my teeth
I must tame myself once again
For a new exile
And this insomnia caused by the absence of
Those I love

Prevents me from falling
Into the trap of tyrants.

My mother prays
For a place in an imaginary paradise
While the muezzin has no profession
Just like the prophets
The day
The war
The fatherland
The assassins and their gods
They too lack professions

Finally comes my father, without work
Alone
In his tomb...

Baghdad-Paris
April 2004

*Originally in Arabic; translated into French by the author and Isabelle Lagny.*

*Author's note from the French edition: Thanks to my friends, Bernadette Lavaud, Marie Didier, and Michel Didier, for their generous contribution to the corrections made during a rereading of the manuscript.*

# POEMS OF BAGHDAD

A selection from the volume of poetry
*The Open Sky of Baghdad*

*Thirty days after thirty years*

Should I not name things
like a hand extended to one who's drowning,
like the unfolding of the seasons?
Have I not said
a thing always finishes at the expense of what's beginning?

A flush of dust wends its way with an odor of childhood
while its procession carries off my uncertainty
slowly
gliding on the mainspring of the day.

I want to come close to you
bring you, in words, what the exile leaves undone

The dawn rises on Baghdad
and it consumes me.

My mother, like the light,
needs no obscurity
just a little silence
when her son, the exile, returns
settles on her branch
in the company of a star tattooed by the fog

For he returns home
like a refugee passing through,
a fugitive looking to share
a smile,
a piece of bread
a corner of a bed
and the witnessing of the drowned twilight.

Baghdad. March 25, 2004

*In the heart of Baghdad*


I

The moon streams over my hand
Tomorrow I'll pull on the thick cord of time
and dawn will break on the traces of the executed

Here
we no longer go hand in hand
and the dew covers a prairie of tombs
astoundingly empty of the dead

In the heart of Baghdad
I plant the forsaken moments of exile
as a dune of stone
presence that skirts the walls of the narrow streets
that one has so wished to erase

Before this crippled city
and the generous men piled into coffins
the assassins from within charge and charge again
with their shameful banners

II

In the heart of Baghdad
I reel
like a mirage

Without eagerness
without elegance
I seize again the illusion of the bedouin
and the hopes congealed in my notebooks

Without fervor
in desiccation and tempest of sand

when a simple show of life defies death
this instant is cold, always.

Baghdad. March 27, 2004

*In the mirror of Baghdad*

Once the dune is passed
the desert belongs to no one
and the sky is wide open.

Baghdad. March 28, 2004

*Nothing in the city*

A frontier drunk with fog and gray men
A very long road, unpaved, where the horizon lingers
No moon tonight
to bring back the faces of my children
no dance in my heart
no seagulls' cry in my memory
no siren's call
no howling of my distress

In this city of a million shrouds
no mirage in your eyes.

Baghdad. April 1st, 2004

*Only the old rug flowered underfoot*

The house had another address
my photo, another place
the table was folded behind the door
my father's chair as well
only the old rug flowered underfoot

I found you at last
in a bare garden
with your large black shawl
your thoughts adrift
cloaked in your prayers
your face
engraved by age

I thought a dying palm was in my arms
Then, in my embrace,
I recognized my mother.

Baghdad. April 2, 2004

## Reflection

In my tears' branches, old mother,
rest your talons

Your warmth has the smile of a mirage
it becomes a bedouin's lover
nourishing an awkward affection
like a hushed wind from a desert door
closed again by a thousand caravans

The sun of Baghdad possesses a cruel pride
as does its memory,
it fragments time
then disappears like snow in Paris...

The exiled is forever alone
with his words of regret,
his wounded love
He's a cry in winter,
an unknown soldier who defies scoundrels

Embedded among words
and my memories of you
I keep watch
by the light of the falling rain
I write to you from within my malaise
like a mother from the depths of her sorrow

No, I'm not frightened
I tell you it is my right to love you
where to say the truth is an act of insurrection

I detest the banners of victory
and the coffins

set down in silence
our eyes captive

I dream of my children on one leg,
standing like storks

And then... there's the other dream
the dream of the stranger
of the executed
the dream of the torturer
the dream of the body
the dream of the word
that spreads each morning's light
into a sheet of discontent
covering what remains of life!

Baghdad. April 6, 2004

*Here, from Baghdad,*
*we say to you that we are alive*

I

I didn't know that the palms, assassinated, would arise again
accompany the prisoners' souls
and walk together toward the day

I say that it's fright
when, in waves, my eyes weave
straw houses
with Baghdad, in the distance
a mirage of fire

I say it's Autumn
when I hoist my skin
strand my writings
without weight or wind

Yes
the sky of Iraq
without Saddam
is blue!

I say it's Spring
in spite of the war among clans
when I anchor the sun
and absurdity makes happiness iridescent

I think sometimes of us,
of that other existence
with which you've papered my home
of that affecting sky
of those memories that are kindled
when I open the notebook of time
of that river that slumbers in the clay

Near the coming of dawn,
and your stormy land
where the thirst to vanquish was to spring
I stepped over your body and the acid sand,
then with violence
the rocky ground seized hold of me

Drawn by the desert
I also wandered along your banks
moving over the immense obscurity of your flesh
and the incandescent silence of prayers

Then the soul, like a stork in the river
moored itself
in the drunkenness of the dune...

I have drunk of your sky until I cry out
I have drowned your wounds in my rough drafts
long governed by distress
by fearful nights

To return or not to return?

I've wandered the multiple days of our existence
my imagining refreshed...

On this invented line, this country of stones
this frontier twisting through a hamlet
along an abandoned road
where pirates cross in the dark
I felt the anguish of the condemned
but there was no door to close against the wind

My only dread,
that night,

was to be lost along the interminable path
never again to see my mother...

I followed the Euphrates and its waters calcinated with
                                        the dead
For a long time, I stirred the cinders
turning them to flames
without forgetting to render the cadavers
and the names of the executed beautiful
Your sky was desert

My being was immersed in the crowd
when your sun purified the houses
and the ruins of the war
And while the soldiers slaked their thirst with our tears
I helped you endure your night of stupefying fever
I ran to you, despite the smoke of the occupier
and the ever-present torture of tyrants
to cover your nakedness with my memory...

And the night suddenly set its body on mine
under the carpet of stars flooding the eye
How will I ever be able to tame this shuddering?
Thus you've known the pangs of death
the drowning of your history and the blood-letting of your
days...

"Yes, from Baghdad, we say to you that we are alive!

"So leave us our crescent moon,
the laughter of the light
and the hair of our women, brushing our face
as they lean over us..."

II

Here I am, Baghdad,
inhabited by the scars of exile
I pass through you, confronting my tormented childhood
my voice inaudible
Perhaps I see standing amid your mirage
a mirage, my love, existing since the god, Shamash[8]
wove his light on your back
incarnate now in the mild heat
that captures the murmur of your headless palms

In your great souk, without geometry
a hamlet in the city's heart
breathing the certainty of spacious things
a dizziness nourishes my passionate, fleeting gaze

Everything is made for man and for light's transparency
in spite of the trace left by days of tears and the imprint
of tyranny.

If you were a woman, Baghdad,
you would be my river of sorrow
and I would know the dying of love

I would at last see your immense eyelids
amid a store of solitude
where no one knows us
but love is learned from taking measure of life
from man's hate
from death as well.

Baghdad-Damas-Paris. April 11, 2004

8 *Sun god in the epic of Gilgamesh*

# AFTERWORD

*Farewell To Arms*

For Sam Hamill

*To be captive, that is not the question*
*The question is not to surrender.* —Nazim Hikmet


Friend, brother from afar
do you hear me?

How can the wisdom of silence be sent to you?

How can a moon be drawn for your eyes
before you lose them looking at such horror?

You, poet of all the continents, I want to honor you during
your lifetime!

You are American and you are my brother,
You are the one my mother endlessly searches for in the
soldiers' faces
You are the one I found like a lament
in a flask stranded in History...

It was at dawn...
It was always at dawn that I dreamed of you
tempestuous steed encircled by the sea,
by wars, by their innocent
And the sky bent over your night with fear.

After that, you had to come as far as my nightmare
shattered by the mockery of assassins.

Tell me, brother from afar,
is it true that we rode side by side under the sky of
Babylonia,

191

your silhouette reflected in Enkidu's eyes?
and I, barefooted, over the dunes?

Who is it among men that has given birth to the monsters
of war?

Silence of the dead, silence about the dead
Silence become ulcerous for cowards

Sam, my brother
Now that your words, adrift, wail in every harbor...
take me into your mirror
when the wounded bird stops short
in the extremity of its pain.

You, orphan of my wandering
I proffer here my condemnation of the Human Comedy
like a game
a brutal idea
that makes me die before the others...

The Euphrates has to lead you to the banks of my exile
and Baghdad, buried in sand, must spread out at your doorstep!

If war is only a vulgar suicide
in the name of what do men die?

We have completed the great register of victims
filled the galley made of shadow.
For those who, returning from forgetfulness,

*Enkidu incarnates the man of earth in the epic of Gilgamesh. He
was created for the pleasure of the gods but in the end escapes,
endangering their realm and becoming a source of anarchy in their
divine world.*

cry searching for solitary vessels
we will be the enraged, "against death,"
an offering to the desert
fishermen of the Tigris beneath the cinders of war
brothers of the throng on the heels of Ben-Laden,
Bush, Sharon, Saddam, and other sharks...

After the devastation of hate,
we'll be brothers who, once more, have found each other
After the consuming of madness,
we'll be the defectors from human stupidity.
Then we'll hope for a perpetual defeat of the bastards
because children continue to die
like birds of the street,
where palm trees are pursued by tanks...

Remember
that morning we passed by my beloved Baghdad,
we found the prophets, their throats slit, on its threshold
and the moon,
near death!

And before our hands knocked at its door
We wept, then wept again...

Since our meeting under the Carovane[9] tent
below the starry sky of Piacenza,[10]
I've followed without respite the enchanted swallow and
the miracle
in the torment of writing.

---

9. Carovane is an Italian association that promotes poetry, primarily
of an antiwar nature.

10. Piacenza was the site of a poetry festival in Italy where the poets
Sam Hamill and Salah Al Hamdani first met.

Yes, my brother in exile,
let us not dream in the other's place,
let us refuse to pick between the good and the bad
among the cadavers!

From high on those cliffs
in terror from the loss of a tomb ravaged by war
my body lying in your arms
like a river,
absorbed your gaze
made of multiple sorrows at the heart of soaring nights.

Brother of harmony, your eye responds to the eye of my
soul,
Your words are sap for my land thirsting for completeness.

Brother from afar
Your words are the sea of a solitary dawn
showering promises.

Friend
take this body of an Iraqi in exile,
with its history and its fears
offer it in sacrifice to the assassins of Mesopotamia, our
mother
like a torment of light riveted to the rain
then tell them there are too many child soldiers here
buried under the starred flag of the night.

Oct. 17, 2003

Curbstone Press, Inc.
is a non-profit publishing house dedicated to multicultural literature
that reflects a commitment to social awareness and change, with an
emphasis on contemporary writing from Latino, Latin American,
and Vietnamese cultures.

Curbstone's mission focuses on publishing creative writers whose work
promotes human rights and intercultural understanding, and on
bringing these writers and the issues they illuminate into the
community. Curbstone builds bridges between its writers and the
public—from inner-city to rural areas, colleges to cultural centers,
children to adults, with a particular interest in underfunded public
schools. This involves enriching school curricula, reaching out to
underserved audiences by donating books and conducting readings
and educational programs, and promoting discussion in the media.
It is only through these combined efforts that literature can truly
make a difference.

Curbstone Press, like all non-profit presses, relies heavily on the
support of individuals, foundations, and government agencies to bring
you, the reader, works of literary merit and social significance that
would likely not find a place in profit-driven publishing channels, and
to bring these authors and their books into communities across
the country.

If you wish to become a supporter of a specific book—one that is
already published or one that is about to be published—your
contribution will support not only the book's publication but also its
continuation through reprints.

We invite you to support Curbstone's efforts to present the diverse
voices and views that make our culture richer, and to bring these
writers into schools and public places across the country.
Tax-deductible donations can be made to:
Curbstone Press, 321 Jackson Street, Willimantic, CT 06226
phone: (860) 423-5110   fax: (860) 423-9242
www.curbstone.org